the
flexible
vegetarian

The Flexible Vegetarian
Copyright © 2017 Quarto Publishing plc
Text copyright © Jo Pratt
Photography copyright © Susan Bell
Cover illustration copyright © Katrin Coetzer
Design: Sarah Allberrey
Commissioning editor: Zena Alkayat

First published in 2017 by Frances Lincoln,
an imprint of The Quarto Group
The Old Brewery, 6 Blundell Street,
London N7 9BH, United Kingdom
www.QuartoKnows.com

A catalogue record for this book is available
from the British Library.

ISBN 978-0-7112-3904-3

Printed and bound in China

9 8 7

Brimming with creative inspiration, how-to projects and useful
information to enrich your everyday life, Quarto Knows is a favourite
destination for those pursing their interests and passions. Visit our
site and dig deeper with our books into your area of interest:
Quarto Creates, Quarto Cooks, Quarto Homes, Quarto Lives,
Quarto Drives, Quarto Explores, Quarto Gifts, or Quarto Kids.

the *flexible* vegetarian

JO PRATT

PHOTOGRAPHY BY SUSAN BELL

F

FRANCES
LINCOLN

Contents

Introduction

Understanding what makes a 'flexible' vegetarian is fairly simple. A flexible vegetarian is someone who wants to cut down on the meat and fish they eat, choosing to have it only on occasions, or maybe only if it's organic. It could also be someone who wants to stop eating meat completely, but still easily cater for meat-eating family and friends. They might want the ingredients in their meals to be more sustainable, kinder to the planet and perhaps even cheaper and healthier. And they want to be able to cook in a flexible way, adding meat and fish when required, but have a store of brilliant, all-vegetarian recipes for every occasion.

Most of my week passes easily, satisfyingly and deliciously meat-free. But every so often I like to flex those 'vegetarian' boundaries. I might be throwing a dinner party where I want to provide for all tastes, or maybe I'm cooking Sunday lunch for the in-laws where meat is a non-negotiable (hi Peter!), or perhaps I need to use up some leftover chicken from that aforementioned Sunday lunch. Sometimes, I might just fancy a bit of salmon myself. That's where the inspiration for this book comes from – for those vegetarian-*plus* moments.

The recipes are designed so that they work alone, or with the addition of meat or fish. You might enjoy the Pearl Barley and Sweet Potato Stew (p110) on Tuesday night, and spice up the rest with some chorizo for Wednesday's lunch. Or make a Sunday brunch of American Pancakes with Tofu 'Bacon' (p21) for you, and real bacon for your partner. There are dishes to suit all occasions, moods, tastes and guests.

All my recipes are also carefully considered for their nutritional balance, without relying on added meat or fish. It's so easy to add protein using pulses, nuts, seeds, soy products, wholegrains, eggs and dairy products, all of which contribute brilliant flavours and textures. There is such an incredible range of vibrant, unusual vegetables and plant-based ingredients on offer in supermarkets, local corner shops or farmers' markets, and I wanted to write a cookbook celebrating these.

Carefully compiled, tried and tested by me, this book is bursting with flavoursome, fulfilling recipes that put vegetables first – with room for a twist. I hope you enjoy cooking them as much as I have writing them!

breakfast / brunch

No day should start without a delicious breakfast, whether you're in a hurry or have time to spare. This chapter is full of filling and bright alternatives to the traditional fry-up, from courgette fritters and tofu 'bacon' to a wholesome quinoa bowl.

soups / broths

I'm a big fan of hearty soups and soul-warming broths, and their ability to serve so many purposes: comfortingly cosy dinners; light, aromatic lunches; tempting bowls to kick-start a dinner party. Pack the veg in with an Italian ribollita (p59), or use cashew nuts as a base for a rich soup (p56). These recipes are miles away from a tired tin of minestrone.

small plates

These dishes are designed to be versatile: serve individually as a starter, as a light meal, as a side, or dish up a tapas-style sharing feast for friends and family.

big plates

These are recipes to wow with. Inspired by cuisines from around the world, there is something here to suit every mood. There are recipes to take your time over – like the Creamy Mushroom, Leek and Chestnut Pie (p102) – and ones you can whip up for a mid-week meal, such as Tray-baked Summer Vegetables with Chilli and Borlotti Beans (p116).

dips / bits

A store cupboard of tricks to keep up your sleeve: colourful dips, unusual pestos, vibrant hummus, an indispensable veg stock, zingy dressings and irresistible nibbles. These are the little extras that will revolutionise your cooking, helpful to have on hand for that final flourish.

Perfectly cooked meat / fish

Meat? In a vegetarian cookbook? Well, yes. It's handy to include some simple and tasty meat and fish ideas that you can serve with your vegetarian recipes as the need arises. These will give you inspiration on flavours and tips for perfect cooking.

The flexible store cupboard

For flexible vegetarian cooking any day of the week, it's good to maintain a well-stocked store cupboard and fridge (including plenty of fresh vegetables). Here are some core staples it's worth keeping in stock.

Beans

For the sake of time and convenience, I use tinned beans most of the time. There is such a huge variety available these days, and they are a fantastic source of protein and fibre; great for bulking out a meal in a similar way to meat.

Cheese

Cheeses are good at providing a variety of flavours and textures, either as a main ingredient or as a seasoning. It's worth mentioning that some cheeses are not strictly vegetarian as they contain animal rennet. Parmesan is the best known one, and is used a fair amount in this book, but there are many vegetarian parmesans available that work just as well, or simply substitute for another hard cheese. You'll see I also use quite a lot of paneer, feta and halloumi – these are all very adaptable vegetarian cheeses.

Eggs

The ultimate convenience food and a powerhouse of nutrition, eggs are one of my favourite ingredients due to their versatility. Opt for free-range or organic, and for the recipes in this book I always use large (unless otherwise stated).

Grains

Forming the body of many vegetarian dishes, these provide both carbohydrate and, in most cases, protein. Keep a good selection in your cupboard so you have them when required. Spelt, freekeh, quinoa, barley, bulgar, faro, couscous, rices, spelt, oats... these are all easily available and have a long shelf life.

Lentils

A very rich source of protein and carbohydrates, lentils come in various colours, shapes and sizes, each with their own uses. Green and brown are great in salads and stews as they usually retain their shape once cooked. Red split and yellow will break down when cooked, creating a paste/purée that makes them a good thickening ingredient in soups, stews and classic Asian dhals. Puy are grown in the French region of Le Puy and are firmer and more flavoursome, making them perfect for braising and using in salads.

Miso paste

Miso paste is the ultimate ingredient for that savoury umami taste (yeasty and salty). It's made from fermented soybeans and can be used to flavour broths, marinades and dressings. Various kinds are available, but the most common are white (sweetest and mildest) and brown/red (richer and stronger).

Nuts and seeds

Packed full of protein, healthy fats, vitamins and minerals, nuts can be utilised in many ways, from mixing into a savoury crumble topping to making cream, dips and pesto.

Smoked paprika

This fantastic spice adds a rich, smoky, almost meaty flavour to recipes. You can get both mild and hot so make sure you know which you are using as the hot one can be pretty fierce!

Tahini

A protein-rich paste made from ground sesame seeds, tahini is best known for its use in hummus. It can also be used in dressings, sauces and as a spread for toast or bagels.

Tofu

Also referred to as beancurd, tofu is derived from soya and a really handy high-protein ingredient. It can be served in numerous ways, from smooth and soft to crisp and crunchy. It can be bought in refrigerated packs or longlife non-refrigerated packs. Alone it's pretty bland, but it has an amazing ability to work well with almost all flavours. Extra firm is best for baking, grilling, frying and stir-fries, while the softer silken tofu works really well blended into sauces, dressings, desserts and smoothies.

Yoghurt / labneh

I am a big fan of labneh (Middle Eastern yoghurt cheese). I have used it a few times in this book. It can be bought from Middle Eastern shops or large supermarkets. It's really simple to make your own with Greek or natural (plain) yoghurt, and you can add herbs or flavourings if you like. It's great to use in wraps, salads, as a dip or in baked potatoes. See page 153 for a labneh recipe.

Vegan alternatives

Milk Unsweetened milks such as nut, oat, rice, soya or coconut milk. There are numerous brands available in shops, but you can also make your own.

Yoghurt Coconut, soya or oat yoghurts are all readily available.

Cream Unsweetened nut, oat or soya creams are becoming more common. Why not have a go at making your own nut cream? See page 56 for a cashew cream recipe.

Vegetarian parmesan Nutritional yeast powder adds a cheesy flavour.

Whole eggs in baking Substitute with chia seeds: simply mix 1 tablespoon of chia seeds with 3 tablespoons of water to replace 1 egg.

Egg whites Substitute with aquafaba (liquid drained from tins of cooked chickpeas). Just whisk until fluffy. Ideal for making pancakes and great in place of the egg white in the Crunchy Wasabi Chickpeas (p159).

breakfast
/brunch

American pancakes
with tofu 'bacon' and maple syrup

Soft, thick and fluffy American-style pancakes are on the menu almost every weekend at my house. Sometimes they'll be served with juicy blueberries and creamy Greek yoghurt, other times sprinkled with cinnamon sugar and sliced bananas. For an occasional treat, I fry up some streaky bacon to serve on top then drizzle the whole lot with maple syrup. I recently had a go at a bacon alternative using tofu, and to my great surprise, it worked brilliantly. Salty, smoky, savoury, slightly sweet and crisp, it has all the traits of bacon, but it's lower in fat. Unlike real bacon, which can be cooked straight from the fridge, this tofu version takes a bit of planning the day before. It's worth it though, as it's just as versatile as bacon and you can use it for many recipes, from a classic 'bacon', lettuce and tomato sandwich, to a wonderfully crumbly topping for soups and salads.

175g/6 oz self-raising flour

1 egg

½ tsp baking powder

300ml/10 fl oz/1¼ cups buttermilk

pinch salt

1 tbsp caster (superfine) sugar

oil, for cooking

maple syrup, to serve

For the 'bacon'

approx. 350g/12 oz firm tofu

125ml/4 fl oz/½ cup soy sauce

1 tbsp tomato purée

1 tbsp maple syrup

2 tsp Marmite

1 tsp sweet smoked paprika

125ml/4 fl oz/½ cup water

Time taken 45 minutes + 8 hours pressing and marinating
Serves 4

First, make the 'bacon'. Drain the tofu of any liquid and sit on a small tray lined with plenty of kitchen paper or clean cloths. Sit another flat tray or plate on top and then sit a heavy weight, such as a couple of books, on top to press out any more liquid from the tofu. Leave for around 4 hours to express any excess liquid. It will be fine to leave it longer.

Slice the pressed tofu really thinly and put into a shallow bowl. Mix together all of the rest of the 'bacon' ingredients and pour over the tofu. Chill in the fridge for about 4 hours to marinate.

To make the pancake batter, simply beat everything together either in a food processor or by hand with a balloon whisk.

Heat a couple of large frying pans over a low–medium heat, one for the pancakes and one for the bacon.

To cook the pancakes, add enough oil to the hot pan to coat the surface. Drop large spoonfuls of the batter into the pan, and leave to cook for around 1–2 minutes until small bubbles start to rise to the surface. Carefully flip over and cook the other side for about 1 minute. You will probably cook three or four in your pan at a time. Continue making the rest of the pancakes, keeping the others warm by sitting on a plate and covering with a tea towel.

Add a trickle of oil to the second frying pan. Drain the tofu from the marinade (it can be used as many times as you like but best to discard after 3–4 days), and pat dry. Fry a few pieces at a time for 1–2 minutes, turning halfway through, until deep golden and crisp.

Serve the fluffy pancakes stacked onto plates with the crisp tofu 'bacon' and plenty of maple syrup poured over.

Flexible
Of course, you can skip making tofu 'bacon' and use real bacon instead.

The green omelette

This omelette works well as a brunch, lunch or light supper, but I think it's a lovely dish to enjoy at the start of your day as it will leave you feeling satisfied, vibrant and ready to hit the day running.

You can use whatever herbs or vegetables you have to hand – just treat this recipe as a guide. The key is to make sure you use the best-quality eggs you can, and avoid overcooking them otherwise they'll resemble rubber. Softly set in the centre, without any colour on the bottom is best.

―――――――――――――――――

2 large handfuls mixed green veg such as
    asparagus, green beans, broccoli, courgette
    (zucchini), spring onion (scallions)
1 tbsp rapeseed or olive oil, plus extra to serve
3 large eggs
handful chopped dill, plus extra to serve
knob of butter
grated zest of ¼–½ lemon
2 tbsp crème fraîche or sour cream
flaked sea salt and freshly ground
    black pepper

Time taken 15 minutes / **Serves** 1

Finely slice the vegetables into slim pieces. Heat the oil in a frying pan over a medium heat and sauté the veg until they are softened and almost golden.

Meanwhile, crack the eggs into a bowl. Add the dill, salt and a little black pepper and whisk with a fork. Heat a small non-stick omelette pan over a medium–high heat and add the butter. When the butter is bubbling, swirl around the pan then add the egg mixture. Use the back of the fork to move the eggs around in the pan until they are setting. Flatten over the surface of the pan and leave to cook for about 1 minute, until the eggs are softly set on the surface.

Mix the lemon zest, crème fraîche, salt and pepper into the sautéed green veg, and spoon on top of the eggs. Using a spatula, fold over one half and slide onto a plate.

Finish with a twist of black pepper, a drizzle of oil and a sprinkle of lemon zest and dill.

Flexible
Fish and seafood are both the perfect match to the dill and lemon in this omelette, so try a couple of slices of smoked salmon torn into pieces, a handful of cooked tiger prawns or 50g / 1¾ oz delicate fresh white crab meat added to the filling.

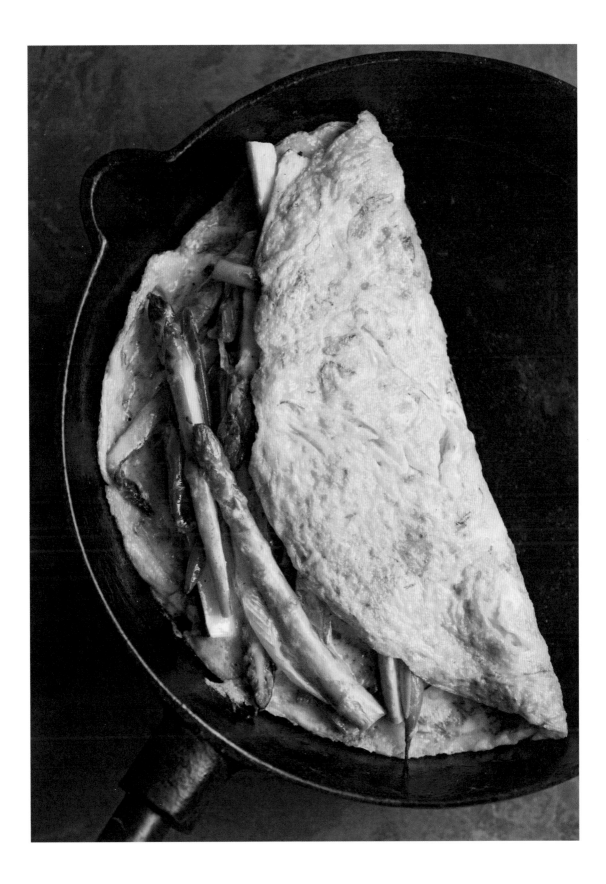

Miso mushrooms on toast

A simple mix of mushrooms is elevated in this dish, which has a satisfying umami flavour. It's a great recipe as it stands, but I'll often serve the mushrooms topped with a fried or poached egg together with some wilted spinach – it makes for a more substantial meal, perhaps a lunch or supper rather than brunch.

---

approx. 250g/9 oz mixed mushrooms, such as shiitake, oyster, portabella, chestnut

1 tbsp olive oil

25g/1 oz butter

2 cloves garlic, peeled and crushed

2–4 slices bread, such as sourdough, rye, seeded or bloomer

1 heaped tbsp white miso paste

4 tbsp cream or crème fraîche

pinch dried chilli flakes

soy sauce, to season

handful chopped parsley

freshly ground black pepper

pickled ginger, to serve

Time taken 15 minutes / **Serves** 2

Clean any dirty mushrooms by brushing off any soil with a pastry brush or wiping with some kitchen paper, and then cut them all into similar sizes. Heat a large frying pan over a high heat and add the oil and butter.

Once the butter has melted and is starting to bubble, throw in the mushrooms. Fry over a high heat, occasionally tossing around until they start to go golden. Towards the end, add the garlic, briefly frying so it doesn't burn in the high heat of the pan.

Meanwhile, toast the bread until lightly golden.

Reduce the heat and add the miso paste, cream and a good splash of hot water, roughly 75ml/2½ fl oz/⅓ cup, to the mushrooms and garlic. Swirl around in the pan until you have a thick creamy sauce. Season with chilli flakes, soy sauce, parsley and a twist of black pepper. Spoon over the toasted bread and serve with some pickled ginger.

Flexible
Grilled smoked bacon served on top of the mushrooms adds even more savoury umami flavour, and a delicious crunch.

Buddha breakfast bowl

A 'buddha bowl' is a hearty nutritious dish made from a stack of healthy ingredients including grains, raw and / or cooked veg, protein, nuts, seeds and dressings. Pile high into bowls (resembling the Buddha's round belly) and you've got yourself a super tasty, balanced meal. Here I've used some of my favourite ingredients that work well served as a brunch, but by all means play around with the flavours, or use up some leftovers such as cooked rice, roasted veg, pulses and green leaves. The recipe includes making flavoured seeds – once these are roasted they'll store for up to 3 weeks in an airtight container, so use what's left over to nibble on throughout the day, sprinkle over salads or roasted veggies, or of course in other buddha bowls another day.

125g/4½ oz mixed seeds (such as linseed, pumpkin, sesame, sunflower and poppy seed)

2 tsp soy sauce

2 tsp agave syrup

2 tsp ras-el-hanout (North African spice mix)

extra virgin olive oil

150g/5½ oz quinoa

375ml/13 fl oz/1½ cups vegetable stock

4 eggs

1 large courgette (zucchini), coarsely grated

finely grated zest and juice of ½ lemon

small handful mint leaves, chopped

3 tbsp tahini

4 tbsp natural (plain) yoghurt

2 large ripe avocados, peeled and sliced

4 tsp harissa paste

flaked sea salt and freshly ground black pepper

Time taken 40 minutes / **Serves** 4

Heat the oven to 160°C/315°F/gas 3.

Mix together the seeds, soy sauce, agave syrup, ras-el-hanout and 1 teaspoon of olive oil. Spread on a baking sheet and bake for 15–20 minutes until golden, shaking the tray halfway through. Remove and leave to cool.

To cook the quinoa, heat a medium saucepan over a high heat. Add the quinoa and toast in the pan for about 30 seconds. Shake the pan to avoid it catching. Pour in the stock and allow to boil for 1 minute. Reduce the heat to low. Cover with a lid and leave to cook for 10 minutes. After this time, turn off the heat and leave for 5 minutes before taking off the lid and running a fork through the quinoa to separate the grains.

Bring a pan of water to the boil and add the eggs. Return to a simmer and cook for 7 minutes for a firm white and slightly soft yolk. Remove from the pan and when cool enough to handle, peel and cut in half lengthways.

Toss the grated courgette in the lemon zest and juice, with the mint, a glug of olive oil and some salt and pepper.

Mix the tahini and yoghurt together and season with a pinch of salt. Loosen with a splash of water so you have the thickness of double cream.

To serve, spoon the quinoa into bowls and top with the courgette, sliced avocado, eggs, a spoon of the tahini yoghurt, a small spoon of harissa and finish with a good sprinkle of the toasted seeds.

Flexible
The options are endless here as the whole point of these bowls is to be flexible about the ingredients you combine. For a breakfast or brunch bowl I quite like to add smoked salmon, smoked trout or smoked mackerel – you can buy these ready to flake straight into the bowl.

Smoked bean and mushroom quesadillas

Quesadillas are the ultimate homemade fast food – they are wonderfully quick and easy to make using just a few ingredients. The basic idea behind the Mexican quesadilla is to put some filling between a couple of tortilla wraps and fry / toast both sides in a pan. Having some cheese inside helps them to stick together as it melts. However, rather than using too much cheese, I like to bulk them out with mashed butter beans and fried mushrooms, along with some other tasty ingredients to make the finished quesadilla utterly delicious, nutritious and thoroughly satisfying.

---

olive oil

300g/10½ oz mushrooms (any type you have are fine such as chestnut, portabella, button), chopped into small pieces

3 cloves garlic, peeled and crushed

2 x 400g/14 oz tins butter beans, drained

2 roasted red (bell) peppers, finely sliced or chopped

½ tsp smoked paprika

large handful chopped parsley

8 flour tortillas

150g/5½ oz grated cheddar and mozzarella mixed

flaked sea salt and freshly ground black pepper

Time taken 25 minutes / **Serves** 4

Heat a large frying pan over a medium–high heat and add a glug of olive oil. When the oil is hot, throw in the mushrooms and fry until they are golden and soft. Stir in the garlic and season with salt and pepper. Cook for a further minute or so, then remove from the heat.

Roughly mash the butter beans with the red pepper, smoked paprika, parsley, a splash of oil and season with salt and pepper.

Sit four tortillas flat on the surface and divide the beans between them. Spread out to the edges. Spoon over the mushrooms, then scatter the cheese on top. Top with the final four tortillas and flatten with the palm of your hand.

Wipe the frying pan with kitchen paper and set over a low heat. Add a drizzle of oil and cook the quesadillas one at a time, for a couple of minutes on each side until golden, carefully turning over with a spatula. If you find it easier, flip it over on a plate before tipping back into the pan to cook the other side.

Cut into wedges and serve hot.

Flexible

It's easy to make a vegetarian and non-vegetarian batch of quesadillas. Stick to the main recipe, and when you're building the quesadillas add some leftover roast chicken, pulled pork or shredded ham to half of them. If you don't have leftovers, around 40g / 1½ oz diced chorizo per person is also great. If you don't mind making a meaty batch of quesadillas, fry the chorizo with the mushrooms, and cut out the smoked paprika in the recipe.

Paneer and turmeric corncakes
with roast mushrooms, tomato and poached eggs

A colourful dish packed with flavour that will wake up your taste buds. The mushrooms and tomatoes are simply roasted until juicy and tender – it's the corncakes that give the big hit of spice. Turmeric, ginger, cumin, fresh coriander and spring onion are all combined with crumbly paneer cheese and sweetcorn to make these corncakes the star of the show.

---

4 large flat or portabella mushrooms

4 ripe tomatoes, halved

olive oil

225g/8 oz paneer cheese, grated

150g/5½ oz sweetcorn

4 tbsp plain (all purpose) flour

2 spring onions (scallions), finely chopped

1cm/½ inch piece ginger, peeled and grated

2 tsp ground turmeric

½ tsp ground cumin

small bunch coriander (cilantro), roughly
chopped

6 eggs

2 tbsp white wine or malt vinegar

flaked sea salt and freshly ground
black pepper

Time taken 30 minutes / **Serves** 4

Heat the oven to 200°C/400°F/gas 6.

Sit the mushrooms and tomato halves in a roasting tray. Drizzle fairly generously with olive oil and season with salt and pepper. Put in the oven to roast for around 20 minutes until the mushrooms are golden and tender, turning the mushrooms over halfway through.

Put the grated paneer, sweetcorn, flour, spring onions, ginger, turmeric, cumin, coriander, 1 teaspoon of salt and a really generous twist of black pepper in a bowl. Lightly beat together two of the eggs and add to the bowl. Mix everything together really well. Using wet hands, divide the mixture into four and shape into thick round cakes.

Heat a medium–large frying pan over a medium heat with enough olive oil to coat the base. Add the corn cakes, and cook for around 3 minutes each side, until golden and firm.

While the corncakes are cooking, bring a pan of water to a simmer. Add the vinegar, then break in the remaining four eggs. Simmer for 3 minutes to poach the eggs.

Place the corncakes on plates, top with a roast mushroom, tomatoes and finish with a poached egg each. Add a twist of pepper, pinch of salt and enjoy.

Flexible
There are a few ways you can be flexible with this recipe. Firstly, you can turn this into even more of an Anglo-Indian brunch by serving fried bacon or sausages on the side. You could also fry some sliced black pudding to serve with the corncakes. Or to make the corncakes themselves a bit different, add 75g/2½ oz thinly sliced ham or pastrami into the mix before shaping and cooking.

Courgette fritters
with smashed avocado and fried halloumi

These are definitely worth getting out of bed for... especially if you're feeling a little worse for wear after a good night out. All the boxes are ticked: there's something a little salty, a little spicy, something fried, lots of healthy nutrients, and it's satisfying, comforting and nourishing.

To make the fritters nice and fluffy on the inside and crisp on the outside, I salt the grated courgette first and leave it for 10–20 minutes before squeezing out excess water. If you haven't got the time or patience, then just mix everything together – but do make sure you cook the fritters immediately before the courgette starts to become wet and soggy.

---

3 medium courgettes (zucchini) (approx. 500g/1 lb 2 oz)

2 ripe avocados

juice of 1 lime

1 red chilli, finely chopped

40g/1½ oz plain (all purpose) flour

40g/1½ oz polenta or fine semolina

1 tsp baking powder

3 eggs, lightly beaten

small bunch mint or coriander, chopped

4 spring onions (scallions), finely chopped

olive oil, for frying

250g/9 oz block halloumi cheese

1 roasted red (bell) pepper, finely sliced

flaked sea salt and freshly ground black pepper

Time taken 50 minutes / **Serves** 4

Coarsely grate the courgettes, put in a sieve over a bowl and toss with ½ teaspoon of salt. Leave for 10–20 minutes, to draw out excess water.

Meanwhile, peel the avocado and put the flesh into a bowl with the lime juice, chilli, a pinch of salt and some black pepper. Smash with the back of a fork and set aside.

Using your hands, squeeze out the water from the courgettes and put them into a mixing bowl. Add the flour, polenta, baking powder, eggs, mint or coriander and spring onions. Mix together to form a batter and season lightly.

Heat two frying pans. Keep one dry, but add a good splash of olive oil to the other, enough to generously cover the surface. Add large spoonfuls of the fritter mixture into the hot oil and flatten lightly with a spatula. Cook for a couple of minutes until golden before turning over and continuing to cook for a further couple of minutes. Repeat with the remaining fritter mix.

Thinly slice the halloumi and add to the dry frying pan. Cook until golden on one side, which will take about 1 minute, then flip over and repeat on the other side.

Serve the fritters onto plates with the fried halloumi, a generous spoonful of smashed avocado, and red pepper slices.

Flexible
Swap the halloumi for the same quantity of smoked salmon or, one of my favourites, crisp, fried chorizo.

Kedgeree
with crispy shallots

Kedgeree is often thought of as a traditional British breakfast, but it actually started off as a humble Indian dish of rice and lentils called 'khichari'. When it made its way to Victorian Britain, smoked fish was introduced along with numerous other adaptations over time, including omitting the lentils and adding cream, butter and eggs. I've moved closer to the original recipe and reintroduced some lentils, but I'm also using coconut milk rather than cream, which lifts the flavour of the whole dish.

_____

60g/2¼ oz puy lentils

200g/7 oz basmati rice

50g/1¾ oz butter

1 onion, finely chopped

1 green chilli, deseeded and finely chopped

2cm/¾ inch piece ginger, peeled and grated

1 tbsp mustard seeds

1 heaped tbsp mild curry powder

400ml/14 fl oz tin light coconut milk

2 shallots

1 tbsp cornflour

sunflower oil, for frying

4 eggs

1 heaped tbsp chopped dill

1 heaped tbsp chopped coriander (cilantro)

juice of ½–1 lemon

smoked flaked sea salt (standard sea salt
      is fine if smoked is unavailable)

freshly ground black pepper

coriander leaves and dill fronds, to serve

Time taken 45 minutes / **Serves** 4

Put the lentils in a pan of boiling water and cook until tender, according to the pack instructions. Drain, keep warm and set aside.

Wash the rice well under the cold tap to remove excess starch.

Heat a large frying pan over a low–medium heat and add the butter. Once hot, stir in the onion, chilli and ginger. Cook for around 10 minutes until the onion is softened, then add the mustard seeds and curry powder. Continue to cook for a minute or so, then add the rice, stirring around to coat in the spiced butter.

Pour in the coconut milk and 200ml/7 fl oz/scant 1 cup of water. Increase the heat, bring to a boil, cover with a lid, then reduce the heat. Simmer for 12–15 minutes until all of the liquid is absorbed, but the kedgeree has a loose creamy texture.

Slice the shallots into rings and lightly coat in the cornflour. Heat about 5cm/2 inches of oil in a small saucepan, and heat until shimmering. Fry the shallots for about 1–2 minutes to crisp up and become lightly golden. Drain on kitchen paper and sprinkle with salt.

Bring a pan of water to the boil and add the eggs. Return to a simmer and cook for 7 minutes. Remove from the pan and when cool enough to handle, peel and cut into quarters.

Stir the cooked lentils, chopped herbs and lemon juice into the kedgeree. Season with salt and pepper. Spoon onto plates and top with the boiled eggs, herb leaves and fronds and scatter with the crispy shallots.

Flexible
Traditionally, smoked haddock is poached in milk and that milk is then used to cook the kedgeree rice. By all means give that a go as it adds a smoky, fishy flavour throughout the dish. But if you want to include fish in individual portions of the kedgeree, rather than the whole lot, simply poach small fillets of smoked haddock (around 125g / 4½ oz per person) in a separate pan of simmering dairy milk (not the coconut milk used in this recipe). Poach for about 5 minutes until cooked through. For added flavour add black peppercorns and a bay leaf to the milk. Flake the poached haddock on top of individual bowls of kedgeree when serving and top with the herbs, eggs and shallots.

Shakshuka

*Shakshuka – a classic Middle Eastern
breakfast dish – is a go-to recipe that
works well for any meal of the day or
night. It's quick, simple, uses everyday
ingredients, and it's really easy to
scale up or down in quantity.*

*The key to the ultimate shakshuka
is to avoid overcooking the eggs. You
want the whites to be just set and
the yolks to remain runny. Keep the
pan on a low heat and cover with a
lid once you add the eggs, then make
sure you leave it to rest for a couple of
minutes before spooning onto plates.
Serve it with some crusty bread or
charred flatbread to mop up all of the
runny yolk and spicy tomato juices.*

---

3 tbsp olive oil

1 onion, finely sliced

1 green (bell) pepper, diced

1 red (bell) pepper, diced

4 cloves garlic, peeled and crushed

2 tsp paprika

½ tsp cumin seeds

2 tsp harissa paste

2 x 400g/14 oz tins chopped tomatoes

1 tbsp lemon juice

2 tsp caster (superfine) sugar

4–8 eggs, depending on how hungry you are

small bunch coriander (cilantro), roughly
    chopped

100g/3½ oz crumbled feta or
    labneh, optional

flaked sea salt and freshly ground
    black pepper

Time taken 1 hour / **Serves** 4

Heat the olive oil in a large lidded frying pan over a medium heat
and add the onion. Cook gently until golden, then add the diced
peppers. Fry for about 5 minutes or so until they are softened, then
stir in the garlic, paprika and cumin. Cook for a couple of minutes
to release their flavour and aroma.

Stir in the harissa, chopped tomatoes, lemon juice and sugar. Bring
to a simmer and gently cook for about 30 minutes until the sauce
has thickened. Have a taste for seasoning and adjust if necessary.

Make 4–8 (depending on how many eggs you are using) craters in
the sauce and break in the eggs. Season them lightly, then turn
the heat right down, as low as possible. Cover with a lid and cook
for about 5–6 minutes until the egg whites are only just set but
the yolks are still nice and soft. You may need a little longer if you
are doing two eggs per person. Remove from the heat, keeping the
lid on and let it sit for a couple of minutes for the whites to cook a
little more.

Scatter with coriander, and some feta or labneh if you want an
extra savoury boost, and enjoy.

Flexible

*It's not a traditional ingredient to use in
shakshuka, but adding some diced chorizo
in with the onion is really good. Not only
does it give a lovely smoky flavour, but it
enriches the sauce with its vibrant red oil.*

soups
/broths

Cauliflower cream cheese soup
with sweet roast onions

This is a contender for my favourite recipe in the book – just looking at it makes me want to polish off the whole bowl. It's mellow and cheesy and so lovely eaten on its own, but the meltingly soft, sticky, sweet roast onions piled in the middle really make it something super special. It's very difficult to stop at just one bowl, which is why I've made the recipe big enough for eight portions.

50g/2 oz butter

1 onion, chopped

2 cloves garlic, peeled and roughly chopped

1 bay leaf

1 large cauliflower, broken into small florets
    (you need about 800g/1 lb 12 oz florets)

1 baking potato, peeled and chopped

500ml/17 fl oz/2 cups milk

750ml/26 fl oz/3 cups vegetable stock

300g/10½ oz cream cheese

1 tsp English mustard

flaked sea salt and freshly ground
    black pepper

1 tbsp nigella seeds, to serve

For the onions

4 large onions, peeled and each cut into 8

3 tbsp olive oil, plus extra for serving

50g/2 oz butter

handful thyme sprigs

Time taken 1 hour / **Serves** 8

Heat the oven to 200°C/400°F/gas 6.

Put the onion wedges in a large roasting tray. Trickle over the oil, dot with butter and scatter around the thyme sprigs. Bake in the oven for 30–45 minutes until the onions are golden and sticky, turning and basting in the butter a few times.

To make the soup, melt the butter in a large saucepan. Add the onion and cook until it is softened but not coloured. Stir in the garlic, bay leaf, cauliflower and potato. Reduce the heat, cover with a lid and leave to cook for 15 minutes, stirring occasionally. Make sure the vegetables don't brown, and if they are sticking add a splash of water to the pan.

Remove the lid and pour in the milk and the stock. Simmer for 15 minutes, or until the cauliflower and potato are tender and beginning to break up.

Put the cream cheese in a bowl with the mustard and beat with a wooden spoon to give you a whipped cream consistency. Remove the soup from the heat and take out the bay leaf. Stir in around two-thirds of the cream cheese and mustard. Cool slightly and then blitz in a food processor or blender until velvety smooth. You'll probably have to do this in two batches. Season to taste with salt and freshly ground black pepper.

Serve the soup hot with a dollop of the whipped cream cheese, some sweet sticky onions piled in the middle, a sprinkle of nigella seeds and a drizzle of olive oil.

Flexible
Add 75g / 2½ oz diced pancetta to the onions halfway through their cooking time and serve both on top of the finished soup.

Pumpkin and butter bean soup

with sage butter and toasted seeds

Make a large pot of this nourishing soup and dip into it throughout the week for lunch or supper. Roasting the pumpkin with some onion, carrot and garlic brings out its natural sweetness, and blending with stock and butter beans makes the soup truly moreish. When it comes to serving, I urge you not to skip the sage butter and toasted pumpkin seeds, they are easy to do and really make the soup sing.

approx. 1.25kg/2 lb 12 oz pumpkin, peeled, giving you approx. 750g/1 lb 10 oz flesh

1 large carrot

1 large onion

3 cloves garlic, peeled

olive oil

2 tbsp pumpkin seeds

400g/14 oz tin butter beans, not drained

1½ litres/2½ pints/6 cups vegetable stock

flaked sea salt and freshly ground black pepper

For the sage butter

50g/1¾ oz butter

about 6 large sage leaves, finely chopped

squeeze of lemon juice

Time taken 1 hour 20 minutes / **Serves** 6–8

Heat the oven to 200°C/400°F/gas 6.

Cut the pumpkin, carrot and onion into similar size chunks. Put into a roasting tray along with the garlic. Add a good glug of olive oil, season with salt and pepper and toss around to coat in the oil. Put in the oven for about 30–40 minutes until the vegetables are tender and becoming golden.

While the veg are roasting, heat a small frying pan over a medium–high heat. Add the pumpkin seeds and toss around in the pan until they are becoming golden and starting to pop. Season with a little salt and set aside.

Remove the roasting tray from the oven and put over a high heat on the hob. Add the beans and their liquid and pour in the stock. Bring to the boil and reduce to a simmer. Cook for 5 minutes.

Transfer the soup to a blender or liquidiser, working in batches, and blitz the soup until it's smooth. Add some more stock if the soup is too thick and season with more salt and pepper if needed, then spoon into bowls.

To make the sage butter, melt the butter in a hot frying pan and once it is foaming, throw in the chopped sage and fry for a few seconds. Remove the pan from the heat, add the lemon juice and then immediately spoon into each bowl of soup. Scatter over some pumpkin seeds and serve straight away.

Flexible

Fry 50g / 1¾ oz thinly sliced smoked bacon or pancetta in a trickle of olive oil in a small frying pan until starting to brown. Add the pumpkin seeds and continue to fry until the bacon and seeds are nicely golden. Drain on kitchen paper and scatter over the soup to serve.

Roast corn chowder
with spiced maple corn

Rich, creamy, smoky and filling. This is my version of a vegetarian chowder that's full of flavour and will keep you satisfied for hours. The spiced maple corn isn't a necessity, but it's a really tasty 'crouton' to scatter over the top, providing you've not eaten it all before serving… it's very hard to resist!

---

2 cobs of corn

olive oil

50g/1¾ oz butter

1 stick celery, thinly sliced

1 medium leek, washed and thinly sliced

1 tsp sweet smoked paprika

1 sprig thyme

1 bay leaf

1 tbsp plain (all purpose) flour

750ml/26 fl oz/3 cups milk

1 medium potato, peeled and diced
   into 1–2cm cubes

pinch dried chilli flakes

2 tsp maple syrup

1 heaped tsp Dijon mustard

1 tbsp roughly chopped parsley

squeeze of lemon juice

flaked sea salt and freshly ground
   black pepper

Time taken 1 hour / **Serves** 4

Heat the oven to 200°C/400°F/gas 6. Put the corn in a roasting tray and lightly rub all over with olive oil. Season with salt and pepper, then put in the oven for 30 minutes, turning occasionally until tender and becoming nicely golden. When cooked, leave until cool enough to handle, then slice off the corn kernels with a sharp knife.

Melt three-quarters of the butter in a saucepan and add the celery, leek, smoked paprika, thyme and bay leaf. Gently cook for about 10 minutes until the celery is tender.

Stir in the flour, cook for about 30 seconds before adding the milk, potato and three-quarters of the roasted corn. Bring to a gentle simmer and cook for 10 minutes until the potato is tender but still just holding its shape.

Meanwhile, heat a small frying pan with the remaining butter. Add the reserved corn, chilli flakes and maple syrup. Cook for about 1 minute or so to coat the corn in the bubbling, sticky syrup, then remove from the heat. Tip onto a parchment-lined tray and leave to cool.

Remove the bay leaf and thyme stalk from the chowder, then stir in the mustard, parsley, squeeze of lemon, salt and pepper. Taste for seasoning, then serve the chowder with some spiced maple corn scattered on top.

Flexible

For a seafood chowder, bring 200ml / 7 fl oz / 1 scant cup of white wine, 1 crushed clove of garlic and a small bunch of parsley to the boil in a large saucepan. Add 500g / 1 lb 2oz of fresh clams, cover with a lid and cook for a couple of minutes, until the shells open. Strain and scatter the cooked clams over the top of the cooked chowder (discard any clams that don't open).

Spinach soup
with lemon and garlic crumbs

You've only got to look at this soup and you can imagine your muscles growing like a certain cartoon character. Spinach can often have a slightly bitter, metallic taste when overcooked, so I add it right at the end of this recipe, giving it a chance to just wilt before blending. Doing this also retains the vibrant green colour of the leaves.

40g/1½ oz butter

1 leek, sliced

1 bunch spring onions (scallions), chopped

1 stick celery, finely sliced

1 medium baking potato, peeled and
    thinly sliced

1 bay leaf

1 litre/1¾ pints/4 cups vegetable stock

500g/1 lb 2 oz spinach leaves

100g/3½ oz crème fraîche, optional

flaked sea salt and freshly ground
    black pepper

For the crumbs

2 dry/stale pieces white bread

1 clove garlic, peeled

finely grated zest of 1 lemon

olive oil

25g/1 oz finely grated parmesan cheese or
    vegetarian equivalent

Time taken 30 minutes / **Serves** 6–8

Heat the butter in a large saucepan and gently sauté the leek, spring onions, celery, potato and bay leaf for a couple of minutes. Cover with a lid and gently cook for about 10 minutes to soften but not colour. Stir once or twice to prevent the veg sticking to the base of the pan.

Pour in the stock and bring to a simmer, cover with the lid and cook for 5 minutes or so until the potato is completely tender.

Meanwhile, put the bread, garlic and lemon zest in a food processor and blitz to a crumb. Heat a glug of olive oil in a frying pan and when it's hot, fry the crumbs, tossing around in the pan until golden. Add the parmesan, season with salt and set aside.

Stir the spinach into the soup pan, a little at a time, so that it can wilt. Season with salt and pepper, remove the bay leaf, then blitz the soup until it's smooth and vibrant green.

Stir in the crème fraîche, if using, and serve with the lemon and garlic crumbs scattered over the top.

Flexible
Add a salty punch to the crumbs by blending 2–3 anchovy fillets with the bread, garlic and lemon. Fry as above and enjoy.

Roast beetroot soup
with parsnip and horseradish

You certainly want to make sure your blender has a secure lid when blitzing this soup, as the last thing anyone would want is a vibrant pink/purple explosion in the kitchen! As well as having an incredible colour, this nutritious soup tastes great, is really simple to make and once cooked can be served hot or chilled.

750g/1 lb 10 oz raw beetroot

400g/14 oz parsnips, peeled and quartered

few sprigs thyme

6 cloves garlic, unpeeled

olive oil

2 tbsp horseradish sauce

5 tbsp sour cream

1 litre/1¾ pints/4 cups vegetable stock

1 tbsp red wine vinegar

1 tbsp agave syrup or honey

flaked sea salt and freshly ground
    black pepper

1 tbsp chopped chives, to serve

Time taken 1 hour 15 minutes / **Serves** 6–8

Heat the oven to 200°C/400°F/gas 6.

Wash the beetroot well, trim the stalks and cut each one into quarters. Sit in a roasting tray with the parsnips, thyme and garlic. Season with salt and pepper, then drizzle with enough oil to lightly coat everything. Cover with foil and roast in the oven for 50 minutes–1 hour, or until the beetroot is tender when pierced with a skewer.

Meanwhile, mix together the horseradish and sour cream. Season and set aside.

When cooked, transfer the beetroot and parsnips to a blender. Squeeze the roasted garlic flesh out of its skin, and add to the blender with the stock, red wine vinegar and agave/honey. Blend until completely smooth. Season with salt and pepper.

If you are serving it hot, put in a saucepan and gently bring to a simmer. Season with salt and pepper. Serve with a dollop of the horseradish sour cream and scatter with chives.

Flexible
Serve this soup with warmed blinis topped with some of the horseradish sour cream and either small slices of smoked salmon or rare roast beef.

Carrot, coconut and cardamom soup

This wonderful soup is packed with aromatic spicy flavour and is perfect for separating into portions for your freezer. You'll be glad of it when all you want is an instant, comforting, healthy lunch.

---

10 cardamom pods, lightly crushed

½ tsp cumin seeds

¼ tsp dried chilli flakes

2 tbsp olive oil

750g/1 lb 10 oz carrots, washed and
    coarsely grated

1 stick celery, finely sliced

15g/½ oz piece ginger, peeled and grated

125g/4½ oz split red lentils

2 x 400ml/14 fl oz tins coconut milk

700ml/1¼ pints/2¾ cups hot vegetable stock

flaked sea salt and freshly ground
    black pepper

small handful coriander (cilantro) leaves,
    to serve

coconut flakes, lightly toasted, to serve

Time taken 40 minutes / **Serves** 6

Split open the cardamom pods and crush the seeds in a pestle and mortar or simply with the flat of a large knife.

Heat a large saucepan and then add the crushed cardamom seeds, cumin seeds and chilli flakes. Dry fry for a minute or so until they release their aroma.

Add the oil to the pan, stir in the carrots, celery and ginger. Stir around for a couple of minutes, then add the lentils, coconut milk and stock. Bring to a simmer and cook for about 20 minutes, covered with a lid, until the lentils are tender.

Blitz the soup until smooth and creamy. Season to taste with salt and pepper. Spoon into bowls and scatter with a few coriander leaves, a twist of pepper and a pile of toasted coconut flakes.

Flexible
Pan fry a few prawns and sit them on top of the soup when serving – this makes it more of a hearty meal, and their delicate sweetness works really well with the aromatic flavours.

Celeriac and butter bean soup
with truffle-popcorn croutons

It may not be the prettiest of vegetables, but when peeled and cooked, celeriac has the most amazing flavour. Similar to celery, but with a sweet, nutty taste, it goes really nicely with the mellow creaminess of butter beans. If you want to create a real talking point, you can spruce up your soup by scattering some truffle and cheese-flavoured popcorn over the top. The popcorn is really easy to make and tastes unbelievably good.

---

2 tbsp olive oil

25g/1 oz butter

1 onion, chopped

1 celeriac, peeled and diced into approx.
    2½cm/1 inch pieces

2 cloves garlic, peeled and crushed

1 bay leaf

1 litre/1¾ pints/4 cups vegetable stock

400g/14 oz tin butter beans, drained

flaked sea salt and freshly ground
    black pepper

For the popcorn

sunflower oil

40g/1½ oz popping corn

25g/1 oz finely grated parmesan cheese
    or vegetarian equivalent

1 tbsp truffle oil

flaked sea salt

Time taken 40 minutes / **Serves** 4–6

Put the oil and butter in a medium–large saucepan over a gentle heat. When the butter has melted, add the onion and sauté for about 5 minutes until it is starting to soften but not colour.

Stir in the celeriac, garlic and bay leaf. Continue to cook for just a few minutes before adding the stock and butter beans. Increase the heat, bring to the boil and cover with a lid. Reduce the heat and gently simmer for 15–20 minutes until the celeriac is completely tender.

Remove the bay leaf, cool slightly and blend until you have a completely smooth, creamy soup. If the soup seems too thick, add some more stock, or even a splash of milk. Season with salt and pepper.

To make the popcorn, put a medium saucepan over a high heat. Once it's hot, add just enough oil to cover the surface (about 2 tablespoons should be plenty). Stir in the corn, coat in the hot oil, then cover the saucepan with a lid. Wait for the popping to start, then shake the pan a few times over the next minute or so until the popping stops.

Remove the pan from the heat. Transfer to a bowl, scatter over the parmesan, a pinch of salt and drizzle over the truffle oil. Toss well to combine.

Spoon the soup into bowls and scatter some popcorn on top of each one, offering any extra popcorn separately.

Flexible
Stir shredded ham hock through the cooked soup and gently warm until heated through. A good handful per person should be plenty.

Miso courgette noodle broth

When I crave a light, refreshing broth, I turn to this every time. It's packed with bright flavours and is pretty speedy to make too. I don't use my spiraliser for many things, but for this I dust it off and give it a go. Using courgette noodles is a lighter alternative to using egg, wheat or rice noodles in the broth, but if you want to bulk it out then by all means forget the courgette and use real noodles instead.

---

3 tbsp unsalted peanuts

1½ litres/2½ pints/6 cups vegetable stock

6 tbsp white miso paste

2 cloves garlic, peeled and crushed

2½cm/1 inch piece ginger, peeled and grated

1 red chilli, finely sliced

3 courgettes (zucchini)

4 spring onions (scallions), finely sliced

150g/5½ oz silken tofu, drained and diced

1½ tbsp rice vinegar

Time taken 20 minutes / **Serves** 4

Place a small pan over a medium heat. Add the peanuts and toss around until lightly golden. Tip onto a board and roughly chop. Set aside to use when serving.

Bring the stock to the boil in a large saucepan over a high heat, then add the miso paste, garlic, ginger and chilli. Reduce the heat, stir until the miso has dissolved and leave to gently simmer for 5 minutes.

Use a spiraliser or julienne peeler to make the courgette noodles. Alternatively, use a vegetable peeler to give you wider strips, more like pappardelle pasta ribbons. Add the courgette to the pan along with the spring onions, tofu and rice vinegar. Allow the noodles to warm through for a minute or so, then divide into bowls. Scatter with the peanuts and serve.

Flexible
Shredded, cooked chicken or pork are a nice addition to this broth. You can also stir in 150–200g/5½–7 oz raw, peeled prawns, allowing them to cook in the broth for a couple of minutes until they turn pink.

Cream of cashew and mushroom soup

I've given the good old cream of mushroom soup recipe a modern-day overhaul. The key to getting the best out of your mushrooms is to cook them over a high heat rather than letting them cook slowly, which is when they become stewed and soggy. The creaminess in this soup comes from making a brilliant cashew nut cream, which makes the soup taste out of this world. Once you've tried it, I think you'll be quite taken with it and start adding it to other recipes too as an alternative to dairy cream.

125g/4½ oz cashew nuts

50g/1¾ oz butter

1 onion, sliced

2 cloves garlic, peeled and crushed

½ bunch thyme, plus extra leaves to serve

1 bay leaf

750g/1 lb 10 oz mixed mushrooms, sliced into similar sizes

750ml/26 fl oz/3 cups vegetable stock

1 tbsp sherry vinegar

flaked sea salt and freshly ground black pepper

olive oil, to serve

Time taken 1 hour + overnight soaking / **Serves** 4–6

Put the cashew nuts in a bowl and cover with cold water. Leave to soak and soften overnight, then drain, rinse well and tip into a blender with 250ml/9 fl oz/1 cup of fresh cold water. Blitz thoroughly until you have a smooth and creamy consistency.

Melt the butter in a large saucepan over a medium heat. Sauté the onion, garlic, thyme sprigs and bay leaf for about 10 minutes until the onions are golden and starting to caramelise. Season with salt and pepper.

Add the mushrooms and cook over a medium–high heat for about 10 minutes until any liquid from the mushrooms has pretty much cooked away.

Pour in the stock, bring to a simmer and cook uncovered for 10 minutes.

Remove the thyme sprigs and bay leaf. Blend the soup in a food processor or liquidiser until smooth. Add two-thirds of the cashew cream and the sherry vinegar. Give the soup a final blitz and check for seasoning, adding extra salt and pepper if needed.

Spoon into bowls and add a swirl of cashew cream, a scattering of thyme leaves and a drizzle of olive oil to serve.

Flexible
Fry around 50g / 1¾ oz sliced black pudding and serve crumbled on top of the soup. The flavours of the earthy black pudding and mushrooms, the creamy cashew nuts and the kick from the sherry vinegar really complement each other.

Spelt ribollita

Ribollita is a rustic Italian soup that makes use of beans, veg and dry (stale!) bread. It's known for being economical, filling and tasty. I've decided to ring the changes by swapping the bread for pearled spelt – it not only adds a healthier edge with extra fibre and protein, but also gives the stew a good texture. If you're particularly hungry, this recipe can serve two as a hearty main course, perhaps with some fresh bread.

---

olive oil

1 large onion, finely chopped

1 large carrot, finely chopped

1 stick celery, finely chopped

4 cloves garlic, peeled and crushed

1 bay leaf

pinch dried chilli flakes

½ tsp fennel seeds, crushed

80g/2¾ oz pearled spelt

3 ripe plum tomatoes, chopped

600ml/21 fl oz/2½ cups vegetable stock

400g/14 oz tin cannellini beans, drained

100g/3½ oz kale, cavolo nero or savoy cabbage,
    tough stalks removed and finely sliced

flaked sea salt and freshly ground
    black pepper

extra virgin olive oil, to serve

parmesan cheese or vegetarian equivalent
    (optional), to serve

Time taken 50 minutes / **Serves** 4 as a light meal, 2 for dinner

Heat a large saucepan with a glug of olive oil over a medium heat. Sauté the onion, carrot, celery, garlic and bay leaf for around 10 minutes until softened.

Stir in the chilli flakes, crushed fennel seeds, spelt, tomatoes, stock and beans. Bring to a simmer, loosely cover with a lid and cook for 20 minutes, until the spelt is tender.

Stir in the kale or whichever greens you are using and return to a simmer. Cook for 10 minutes, adding extra stock if needed. Season with salt and freshly ground black pepper.

Stir in a good glug of extra virgin olive oil and spoon into bowls, scattering with some grated parmesan if you like.

Flexible
Start by frying around 100g/3½ oz diced, smoked pancetta, bacon or chorizo at the very beginning of this recipe. Allow it to become lightly golden before adding the onion, carrot and other ingredients.

Aubergine and green bean laksa

Slurp and sip this fragrant and spicy Malaysian broth when you're feeling a little under the weather, or just want to take the weight of the world off your shoulders. The paste can be made ahead of time and stored in the fridge for up to one week.

400ml/14 fl oz tin coconut milk
500ml/17 fl oz/2 cups vegetable stock
1 large or around 350g/12 oz baby aubergine
   (eggplant)
200g/7 oz green beans
75g/2½ oz dried thin rice noodles
mint or coriander (cilantro) leaves, to garnish

For the laksa paste
2 red chillies, roughly chopped
2 cloves garlic, peeled
2cm/¾ inch piece ginger, peeled and
   roughly chopped
1 stalk lemongrass, tough outer layer removed
   and roughly chopped
½ tsp turmeric
4 lime leaves, finely shredded
small bunch coriander (cilantro), roughly
   chopped
2 tbsp peanut butter
2 tbsp sunflower oil
1 tsp flaked sea salt

Time taken 45 minutes / **Serves** 4

Put all of the laksa paste ingredients into a small blender and blitz to a paste. Add a splash of water if the ingredients are not coming together well.

Heat a wok or saucepan over a medium–high heat. Fry the paste for a minute or so, stirring continuously, making sure it doesn't burn.

Reduce the heat to low. Stir in the coconut milk and stock and bring to a gentle simmer. Cut the aubergine into small chunks, or if you are using baby ones, cut them in half lengthways. When the laksa is simmering, add the aubergine, return to a simmer and cook gently for 8–10 minutes, or until the aubergine is soft.

Stir the green beans into the laksa and cook until they are tender, around 5 minutes.

Meanwhile, cook the noodles according to the pack instructions, drain and divide between four bowls. Spoon over the laksa and finish by scattering with fresh coriander or mint.

Flexible
To make a prawn laksa, add about 50–75g / 1¾–2½ oz raw, peeled prawns per person into the laksa after you add the beans, allowing them to cook for a couple of minutes until they turn pink. To make a chicken laksa, you can add strips of raw chicken breast into the pan when frying the laksa paste. Alternatively, stir through shredded cooked chicken (leftover roast chicken is ideal) into individual portions of the laksa.

small
plates

Fried pickles with beetroot and dill salad

*I've tried various types of gherkins
and pickled cucumbers for this recipe,
but I finally found that the best ones
to use are sweet, pickled cucumbers.
Avoid using the really vinegary ones
as they can be too strong. If you can't
buy them as spears, then simply slice
the whole sweet pickled cucumbers
into quarters lengthways before
coating in the crumbs.*

---

sunflower oil, for deep frying

approx. 16 sweet pickled cucumber spears

100g/3½ oz dried breadcrumbs

pinch cayenne pepper

5 tbsp plain (all-purpose) flour

100ml/3½ fl oz/scant ½ cup buttermilk

For the salad

250g/9 oz cooked beetroot (not in vinegar)

1 shallot, finely chopped

small bunch dill, chopped

finely grated zest of 1 lemon

2 tsp lemon juice

3 tbsp sour cream

flaked sea salt

Time taken 20 minutes / **Serves** 4

To make the salad, dice the beetroot and mix together with the
shallot, dill, lemon zest and juice and sour cream. Season with
a pinch of salt and set aside.

Heat a pan of oil, around one-third full, to 180°C/350°F. If you don't
have a thermometer, drop a small chunk of bread into the oil. It will
turn brown in 30 seconds if the oil is the correct temperature.

Pat the pickled cucumber spears dry with kitchen paper. Mix
together the breadcrumbs, cayenne and a pinch of salt. Dust the
pickles in flour, dip them into the buttermilk and then evenly coat
in the breadcrumbs.

Deep fry in batches for 3–4 minutes until golden. Drain on kitchen
paper and serve hot and crunchy with the beetroot and dill salad.

Flexible
*You can fry numerous ingredients in the same crumb.
Strips of raw chicken breast (deep fry for 6–8 minutes),
raw tiger prawns (2–3 minutes) and even sliced avocado
(3–4 minutes) all work well.*

Chinese potstickers
with sweet and spicy dipping sauce

Potstickers are made by filling wonton wrappers with a mix of finely chopped vegetables and / or pork before frying and steaming them in the same pan. They are very similar to Japanese gyoza, and just as fun to make. Be careful not to overfill the wonton wrappers as the filling will split the wrapper when cooking. Wonton wrappers can be bought fresh or frozen from Asian supermarkets or online.

---

1 tbsp sesame oil

3 tbsp groundnut oil

150g/5½ oz shiitake mushrooms,
   finely chopped

2 spring onions (scallions), finely chopped

2 cloves garlic, peeled and crushed

2½cm/1 inch piece ginger, peeled
   and grated

100g/3½ oz tinned water chestnuts, drained
   and finely chopped

75g/2½ oz bamboo shoots, drained and
   finely chopped

small handful coriander (cilantro), finely
   chopped

25–28 wonton wrappers

cornflour, for dusting

For the dipping sauce

2 tbsp soy sauce

1 tbsp rice vinegar

1 tbsp caster (superfine) sugar

½ tsp dried chilli flakes

Time taken 45 minutes / **Serves** 4–6

Heat the sesame oil and 1 tablespoon of the groundnut oil in a saucepan and gently sauté the mushrooms for 5 minutes until softened. Add the spring onion, garlic and ginger, and continue to cook for a further 5 minutes. Transfer to a bowl and add the water chestnuts, bamboo shoots and coriander. Season with salt and leave to cool for 10 minutes or so.

To make the potstickers, lay the wonton wrappers on a clean work surface and cover with a damp tea towel to stop them from drying out. Lightly dust a tray with cornflour and place a small bowl of water alongside it.

Place 1 teaspoon of the filling onto the middle of a wrapper, brush the edges with a little water, then fold the wrapper in half over the filling into a half moon shape. Pinch and pleat the edges to seal, then place bottom-side down onto the flour-dusted tray. Repeat with the remaining ingredients. You should end up with around 25–28.

Heat the remaining 2 tablespoons of groundnut oil in a large non-stick frying pan over a high heat, then add the potstickers, bottom-side down, in a single layer. Reduce the heat to medium and fry for 2 minutes, or until the undersides are golden.

Pour about 1cm/½ inch of water into the pan, bring to the boil, then cover and reduce to a medium–low heat. Simmer for 6–8 minutes, or until the liquid has almost evaporated (if it reduces too quickly, top up with a splash more water halfway through). Remove the lid and fry for a further minute, or until the undersides are crisp.

Combine the dipping sauce ingredients, then serve with the potstickers.

Flexible
Swap the shiitake mushrooms for the same quantity of minced pork or minced chicken, then cook as above.

Gnudi with pea shoot pesto and asparagus

Gnudi are gnocchi-like dumplings made from ricotta and semolina (rather than potato), so are really light in texture. They can appear a little fiddly to make, but you'll soon get into the swing of it – and the end result is worth the effort. I serve these with blanched peas and asparagus, then toss in a super delicious pea shoot pesto. It's light, summery and makes a perfect starter or sharing plate with the Courgette Fritti (p71).

350g/12 oz ricotta cheese

25g/1 oz finely grated parmesan cheese
   or vegetarian equivalent

1 egg yolk

a really good grating of nutmeg

200g/7 oz semolina

250g/9 oz asparagus tips

125g/4½ oz frozen peas

flaked sea salt and freshly ground
   black pepper

For the pesto

75g/2½ oz pea shoots

20g/¾ oz basil leaves

1 clove garlic, peeled and crushed

40g/1½ oz pinenuts

50g/1¾ oz grated parmesan cheese or
   vegetarian equivalent

125ml/4 fl oz/½ cup olive oil, plus extra
   for drizzling

Time taken 40 minutes + 4 hours draining + overnight resting
Serves 4

Line a sieve with a piece of muslin or new J-cloth. Set over a bowl and tip in the ricotta. Gather up the sides of the cloth and tie tightly with string or an elastic band. Leave to drain excess liquid from the ricotta for around 4 hours. Transfer the ricotta to a clean bowl and beat in the parmesan, egg yolk and nutmeg, and season.

Spread the semolina onto a baking tray that fits into your fridge. Roll walnut-size balls of the gnudi mixture in your hands then roll around in the semolina. You should end up with around 24 balls. Press each one lightly with the back of a fork to flatten slightly. Sprinkle some of the semolina over the top of the gnudi and pop in the fridge, uncovered, for around 12 hours to dry out. The longer you leave them the better, as they will stay nice and firm when cooked.

To make the pesto, put all of the ingredients aside from the oil in a food processor and pulse to finely chop together. With the motor running, slowly add the olive oil until you have a smooth pesto. Season with salt and pepper. If you're not using it straight away, cover the surface with a layer of olive oil to prevent discolouration.

Bring a large saucepan of salted water to the boil. Add the asparagus and peas, and cook for 2 minutes. Remove with a slotted spoon and keep warm. Return the water to a simmer and at the same time, heat a large frying pan over a low–medium heat.

Shake off any excess semolina from the gnudi and carefully lower half into the simmering water. Cook gently for 2 minutes, until they rise to the surface. Remove with a slotted spoon and sit in a sieve or colander. Repeat with the remaining gnudi.

Add half of the pesto to the hot frying pan. Add the asparagus, peas and gnudi. Gently toss around to coat in the pesto and serve.

Flexible
Light and delicate, crab is a perfect addition to the gnudi. Lightly dress 100g/3½ oz flaked white crabmeat in a trickle of extra virgin olive oil, squeeze of lemon juice, pinch of salt and twist of black pepper. Scatter over the top of the finished dish as you serve.

Courgette fritti
with goat's cheese and truffle honey

I got the inspiration for these from one of my favourite restaurants in London called Salt Yard, which serves Spanish and Italian style tapas. I just love the combination of lightly battered crisp courgette dipped in creamy goat's cheese and generously drizzled in honey flavoured with truffle oil. I'm pretty sure you'll love them too. Pair with Gnudi with Pea Shoot Pesto and Asparagus (p68) for a lovely lunch.

150g/5½ oz plain (all purpose) flour

3 tbsp olive oil

200ml/7 fl oz/scant 1 cup water

150g/5½ oz soft goat's cheese

50g/1¾ oz cream cheese

1 tsp fresh thyme leaves, roughly chopped

2 tbsp runny honey

2 tsp truffle oil

2 egg whites

4 medium courgettes (zucchini)

sunflower oil, for deep frying

flaked sea salt and freshly ground
   black pepper

Time taken 40 minutes / **Serves** 4

Put the flour in a mixing bowl and pour in 2 tablespoons of olive oil plus a pinch of salt. Whisk in the water until you have a batter the consistency of double cream. Cover and sit in the fridge to rest while you prepare everything else.

Beat together the goat's cheese, cream cheese, thyme leaves and 1 tablespoon of olive oil with an electric whisk until light and airy. Add a pinch of salt if needed and keep chilled until you are ready to serve.

To make the truffle honey, simply mix together the honey and truffle oil. Have a taste, adding more oil if you prefer a stronger truffle flavour.

Cut the courgettes into 1cm/½ inch thick slices or chip shapes.

Whisk the egg whites until they are starting to hold their shape, then fold into the rested batter mix.

Heat a pan or a deep fat fryer no more than one-third full of oil to 180°C/350°F. If you don't have a thermometer, you'll know it's hot enough when a small piece of bread dropped in becomes golden in 30 seconds. Working in batches, dip the courgette pieces into the batter, allowing the excess to drip back into the bowl, then fry in the hot oil for 2–3 minutes until lightly golden.

Drain on kitchen paper before dividing between plates. Add a spoon of the whipped goat's cheese and finish with a generous drizzle of the truffle honey and a twist of black pepper.

Flexible
As well as courgette fritti, you can make sardine fritti. Dip cleaned and deheaded fresh sardine fillets into the batter and deep fry in the hot oil for 2–3 minutes until golden.

Smashed bean, kale and tomato toast

*I mainly work from home and
try to make my lunch as varied
and interesting as possible. I'll
often challenge myself to see what
combinations I can come up with out
of items in the fridge or cupboard, to
top crusty bread. I don't always write
them down, but when I made this
twist on beans on toast, I loved it so
much I thought it would be a shame
not to share it.*

400g/14 oz tin white beans, such as butter,
    cannellini or haricot, drained

½ tsp paprika

1 small clove garlic, peeled and crushed

juice of ½ lemon

3 tbsp extra virgin olive oil

2 handfuls kale leaves

2 or 4 slices (depending on size) ciabatta,
    bloomer or sourdough bread

10 halves of cherry tomatoes, semi-dried
    tomatoes or sun-dried tomatoes

1 tbsp pumpkin seeds, lightly toasted

flaked sea salt and freshly ground
    black pepper

Time taken 15 minutes / **Serves** 2

Put the beans in a bowl and roughly mash with the paprika,
garlic, half the lemon juice, 2 tablespoons of olive oil and some
salt and pepper.

Tear the kale into small bite-size pieces, throwing out any
tough stalks. Put in a bowl and add the remaining lemon juice,
1 tablespoon of olive oil, some salt and pepper, and rub them all
together, breaking down the kale slightly.

Toast the bread on both sides until lightly golden. Spread the
smashed beans onto the toast, top with the kale and arrange
the tomatoes on top. Finish by scattering over the pumpkin
seeds and serve.

Flexible

*You can deconstruct this recipe and turn it into a more substantial meal with the
addition of some pan-fried fish. Make the butterbean mash in the same way and
spoon onto a plate. Scatter the dressed kale and tomatoes over the beans. Then top
with a fillet of pan-fried fish (I think cod works well, see p177 for instructions).
Sprinkle on the pumpkin seeds and drizzle generously with extra virgin olive.
Serve with or without the toasted bread.*

Roast garlic and lemon hummus

Mellow roast garlic and bitter-sweet roasted lemon transforms a basic hummus into something quite special. The flavours work really well for the Watermelon, Tomato and Hummus Bowl (opposite) but it can be enjoyed however you fancy: as a dip with veggies, breadsticks or crackers, spread onto sandwiches, wraps or flatbreads, on toast, in baked potatoes, in salads or even burgers…

—————————————————

1 garlic bulb, peeled

extra virgin olive oil, plus more for drizzling

2 lemons

2 x 400g/14 oz tins chickpeas

5 tbsp tahini

2 tsp flaked sea salt

Time taken 55 minutes / **Serves** 6–8

Heat the oven to 180°C/350°F/gas 4.

Rub the garlic bulb in a little olive oil and loosely wrap in a piece of aluminium foil. Set on a baking sheet.

Cut the lemons in half across the centre and remove any visible pips. Rub with olive oil and sit cut-side down on a piece of foil with the edges curled up to reserve any juices. Place on the baking sheet with the garlic. Put in the oven and after about 25 minutes the lemon should be becoming soft and golden. Lift the lemons and foil off the tray and set aside to cool. Continue roasting the garlic for a further 20 minutes.

When the garlic is cool enough to handle, squeeze out the soft roasted flesh into the bowl of a food processor. Then squeeze in the lemon juice and pulp, removing any stray pips.

Drain the chickpeas over a bowl, reserving the liquid. Add the chickpeas to the food processor along with the tahini, 2 tablespoons of olive oil, the salt and 4 tablespoons of the reserved chickpea liquid. Blitz until smooth. If the hummus is too thick, add more of the chickpea liquid.

Transfer to a bowl and drizzle with some extra virgin olive oil and serve straight away, or store in the fridge for up to 5 days.

Watermelon, tomato and hummus bowl

*I can't get enough of this salad bowl –
it's ideal on a sunny day when I want
to whip up a quick lunch and get back
outside. Your favourite shop-bought
hummus is fine to use, but if you've a
bit more time on your hands then have
a go at making your own. My favourite
with this is Roast Garlic and Lemon
Hummus (opposite), but there are a
couple of other hummus recipes on
p156 that you could use. Alternatively,
curd cheese or soft goat's cheese are
equally good spread around the bowl,
with the sweet, tangy salad in the
centre. (Picture on following page.)*

––––––––––––––––––––

½ small red onion, finely sliced

red wine vinegar

500g/1 lb 2 oz different-coloured and
    sized tomatoes, perfectly ripe

500g/1 lb 2 oz watermelon

handful pitted black kalamata olives, halved

½–1 red chilli, finely sliced

handful mint leaves, roughly chopped

extra virgin olive oil

approx. 300g/10 oz shop-bought or
    homemade hummus

1 tsp sumac

flaked sea salt and freshly ground
    black pepper

Time taken 15 minutes / **Serves** 4

Put the onion in a shallow bowl and pour over just enough red wine
vinegar to cover. Leave to stand while you prepare everything else.
This will take out the 'bite' that raw onion has in salads.

Chop the tomatoes and watermelon into bite-size pieces, removing
any watermelon seeds, and put in a mixing bowl along with the
olives, chilli, mint, a good glug of olive oil and some salt and pepper.
Lift the onions from the vinegar and add to the bowl. Spoon over 1
tablespoon of the vinegar and gently mix everything together. Have
a taste and add more vinegar for a sharper finish or more oil for a
richer dressing.

Divide the hummus between four shallow serving bowls and smear
all around the inside. Spoon the salad into the bowls along with
any dressing/juices in the bottom of the mixing bowl. Sprinkle
with sumac and serve.

Flexible
*You can buy marinated anchovy fillets to mix into this salad – a lovely addition.
Or if you want to make this into a more special meal, then sear four 100g/3½ oz
fresh tuna fillets. First, season and rub the tuna with a little olive oil, then cook
for 1½–2 minutes on each side in a hot frying or griddle pan. Break into chunks
and serve either warm or cool mixed into the salad.*

Halloumi fries
with fattoush

If you've never tried halloumi fries before, then you have to give these a go. Something incredible happens to the cheese when coated in flour and deep-fried: they become very moreish. I know that deep-fried cheese may not be the healthiest recipe, but when served with this crunchy chopped salad you can ease your conscience at least a little bit.

---

sunflower oil, for deep frying

375g/13 oz halloumi cheese

2 tbsp plain (all purpose) flour

1 tsp paprika

½ tsp sumac

For the fattoush

1 pitta bread

extra virgin olive oil

½ cos lettuce

3 ripe tomatoes

¼ cucumber, halved and seeds removed

75g/2½ oz radishes, halved or quartered

3 spring onions (scallions), chopped

small bunch parsley, chopped

small bunch mint, chopped

juice of ½ lemon

2 tbsp pomegranate seeds

1 tbsp pomegranate molasses

4 tbsp natural (plain) yoghurt

flaked sea salt and freshly ground
   black pepper

Time taken 45 minutes / **Serves** 4

Heat the oven to 200°C/400°F/gas 6. Brush the pitta or flatbread with a little olive oil and bake for about 15 minutes until golden and crisp. Cool slightly, then break into small pieces.

Cut the lettuce, tomatoes and cucumber into small irregular chunks and put into a bowl with the radish, spring onions, parsley and mint. Toss with the lemon juice, a good glug of extra virgin olive oil and season with salt and pepper. Set aside while you make the halloumi chips.

Heat a pan or deep fat fryer no more than one-third full of sunflower oil to 180°C/350°F. It will be hot enough when a small piece of bread dropped into it turns golden within 30 seconds.

While the oil is heating, cut the halloumi into chip shapes. Combine the flour and paprika and toss the halloumi in it to coat. Fry in batches for a couple of minutes until golden. Drain on kitchen paper, serve onto plates and sprinkle with the sumac.

Toss the baked pitta into the fattoush and finish by scattering over the pomegranate seeds and drizzling with the pomegranate molasses and natural yoghurt.

Flexible
Add a batch of sardine 'fries' to the halloumi. Dust 8 cleaned and deheaded sardines in the seasoned flour mixture and deep fry in the hot oil for 2–3 minutes until golden.

Pea and carrot pakoras

These spicy little balls are great as a pre-dinner nibble, or a side dish to an Indian meal. You can swap the veg depending on what you have in: sweet potato, squash, swede or celeriac work well instead of carrot. And you can use sweetcorn instead of peas. Serve with the Spicy Roast Cauliflower (p83).

---

2 medium carrots, coarsely grated

150g/5½ oz frozen peas, defrosted

4 spring onions (scallions), finely sliced

1 red or green chilli, deseeded and
    finely chopped

small bunch coriander (cilantro), chopped

1 tsp black mustard seeds

2 tsp garam masala

50g/1¾ oz gram (chickpea) flour

50g/1¾ oz self-raising flour

1 tsp flaked sea salt

sunflower oil, for deep frying

To serve

4 tbsp natural (plain) yoghurt

1 tsp mint sauce

mango chutney

Time taken 25 minutes / **Serves** 4

Put the grated carrot, peas, spring onion, chilli, coriander, mustard seeds, garam masala, both flours, salt and 2 tablespoons of water in a bowl. Mix well until it can be squished into balls. Add more water, a little at a time, if need be.

Heat around 2½cm/1 inch of sunflower oil in a saucepan. When the oil starts to shimmer, or when you drop a small piece of the mixture into the pan and it sizzles, then it's hot enough. Using your hands, shape the mixture into small balls, roughly the size of whole walnuts.

Fry in the hot oil for 2–3 minutes, working in small batches, until golden, turning halfway through. Drain on kitchen paper.

Mix the yoghurt and mint sauce together in a bowl. Serve with the minted yoghurt and/or mango chutney.

Flexible

Minced pork, chicken, beef or lamb can be added to the mixture for a meaty version of the pakoras. You'll need to use around 100g/3½ oz mince and cut down the carrot and corn quantity by half. Thoroughly mix everything together and firmly shape into balls. Cook as above, frying for 3–4 minutes until golden and cooked through.

Spicy roast cauliflower
with fresh mango relish

Cauliflower is a wonder veg: it's great at holding its own when roasted and can absorb plenty of robust spices. I find myself roasting florets a lot, sometimes coated in chilli and coriander and served with a squeeze of lime, and sometimes flavoured with cinnamon, cumin and paprika together with a harissa-laced yoghurt. But more often than not it will be this recipe: coated in a powerful mix of Indian spices and served with a fresh, tangy mango relish. Serve with the Pea and Carrot Pakoras (p80).

----

1 medium head cauliflower

3 tbsp sunflower or groundnut oil

1 tsp garam masala

1 tsp cumin seeds

½ tsp turmeric

½ tsp hot chilli powder

flaked sea salt

For the fresh mango relish

2 tsp sunflower or groundnut oil

1 tsp mustard seeds

½ tsp nigella seeds

1 mango, peeled and finely diced
   (about 5mm–1cm/¼–½ inch)

1 tbsp white wine vinegar

1 tbsp caster (superfine) sugar

¼ tsp chilli powder

Time taken 45 minutes / **Serves** 4

Heat the oven to 200°C/400°F/gas 6.

Break the cauliflower into bite-size florets and put in a large mixing bowl.

In a small bowl, mix together the oil, garam masala, cumin seeds, turmeric and chilli powder. Pour over the cauliflower and toss around to coat. Transfer to the oven and roast for about 30 minutes, tossing the tray a couple of times, until the cauliflower is just tender and becoming golden.

To make the fresh mango relish, heat the oil in a saucepan and add the mustard and nigella seeds. Cook for a couple of minutes until the mustard seeds start popping. Add the remaining ingredients along with 75ml/2½ fl oz/⅓ cup of water, and cook over a gentle heat for 10 minutes, until the mango is cooked through and starting to break down. Remove from the heat and leave to cool slightly.

Serve the cauliflower scattered with sea salt and the mango relish on the side to dip into.

Roast corn and carrot salad
with maple mustard dressing

You can serve this sweet, spicy, crunchy salad as a starter, lunch or accompaniment to a main course. You could also serve with some quinoa or couscous for a more filling dish. I like to use a selection of different-coloured carrots as they look great – many green grocers and supermarkets are now stocking them in season, so do look out for them.

---

4 cobs of corn

500g/1 lb 2 oz carrots, washed and peeled
   if necessary

olive oil

pinch dried chilli flakes

½ tsp ground coriander (cilantro)

75g/2½ oz whole blanched almonds

4 spring onions (scallions), finely sliced on
   an angle

handful fresh coriander, roughly chopped

flaked sea salt and freshly ground
   black pepper

For the dressing

2 tbsp rapeseed oil

2 tsp maple syrup

2 tsp Dijon mustard

2 tsp cider vinegar

Time taken 45 minutes / **Serves** 4

Heat the oven to 220°C/425°F/gas 7.

Put the corn and carrots in a roasting tray and drizzle fairly generously with olive oil. Scatter over the chilli and ground coriander, season with salt and pepper and roast in the oven for 30 minutes, turning frequently until the carrots and corn are cooked and colouring. For the final 10 minutes, add the almonds to the roasting tray, toss in the oil and roast with the vegetables so they take on a nice golden colour.

To make the dressing, put all of the ingredients in a small bowl and season with salt and pepper. Whisk until combined.

When cooked, slice the kernels off the corn with a sharp knife into a large bowl. Cut some of the carrots into smaller pieces if they are particularly large. Add to the sweetcorn along with the almonds, spring onions and fresh coriander. Spoon the dressing all over the salad. Toss everything together gently and serve warm or at room temperature.

Flexible

You can roast a whole chicken to serve with this salad (see p173). Or simply roast individual chicken breasts, preferably with their skin on for a better flavour. Rub in a little olive oil, then season. Roast in a small tray for 25–30 minutes while you roast the carrots. To check the chicken is cooked, pierce the thickest part of the meat with a skewer – the juices should run clear, not pink.

Sweet potato and chipotle bean tacos
with chunky avocado salsa

These tacos are proper feel-good food. Put the toasted tortillas in the middle of the table and everyone can start to pile on the smoky, spiced potato and beans, chunky avocado salsa, fresh coriander, a squeeze of lime and big dollop of sour cream. Eating them with grace is impossible, but no one will care as they'll be too busy getting stuck into their own.

---

2 tbsp olive oil

1 red onion, chopped

1 medium–large sweet potato, peeled and
    diced into approx. 1cm/½ inch pieces

2 cloves garlic, peeled and crushed

1 tsp ground cumin

1 tsp ground cinnamon

1 tbsp chipotle paste

2 tbsp tomato purée

1 x 400g/14 oz tin kidney or black eye
    beans, not drained

flaked sea salt and freshly ground
    black pepper

8 corn tortillas

sour cream, to serve

For the salsa

1 large ripe avocado, peeled and
    roughly chopped

4 spring onions (scallions), finely chopped

2 ripe tomatoes, deseeded and diced

2 limes, cut into wedges

handful chopped coriander (cilantro)

2 tbsp extra virgin olive oil

flaked sea salt and freshly ground
    black pepper

Time taken 40 minutes / **Serves** 8

Heat the olive oil in a large frying or sauté pan. Sauté the onion until softened before adding the sweet potato, garlic, cumin and cinnamon. Cook for a couple of minutes, then stir in the chipotle paste, tomato purée and tinned beans, along with their liquid and around 75ml/2½ fl oz/⅓ cup of water (if you've already drained them, then add around 175ml/6 fl oz/¾cup of water). Season with salt and pepper. Bring to a simmer, cover with a lid and cook on a low heat for about 15–20 minutes, until the potato is cooked and the sauce thickened. Add a splash more water if it seems necessary.

Next, make the salsa. Lightly mix together the avocado, spring onions, diced tomato, juice of half a lime, chopped coriander and extra virgin olive oil. Season with salt and pepper and transfer to a serving bowl.

Heat the tortillas one at a time, either in a hot dry frying pan for 30 seconds–1 minute each side, or by holding over the gas flame until lightly charred on each side.

Spoon some of the sweet potato and chipotle bean mixture over each tortilla, add some avocado mixture and a dollop of sour cream. Squeeze over extra lime and tuck in.

Flexible
Swap the tinned beans for around 250g/9 oz diced chicken breast, pork fillet, beef or lamb steak, adding to the pan with the sweet potato.

Grilled peaches, burrata and mint pesto

This makes twice the amount of pesto you'll need for serving, but it's worth making extra. Use it to serve another day with roasted root vegetables, an alternative to mint sauce with roast lamb, or stirred through risotto or pasta with some fresh peas and asparagus.

If you can get hold of burrata for this recipe it's a real treat – a naughty one at that, as it's rich mozzarella cheese filled with cream. Buffalo mozzarella is a great back-up choice though, and somewhat easier to get hold of in supermarkets.

----

2 or 3 ripe peaches

olive oil

2 x 200g/7oz balls burrata
   (or buffalo mozzarella)

For the pesto

40g/1½ oz mint leaves

40g/1½ oz grated parmesan cheese
   or vegetarian alternative

40g/1½ oz pinenuts

1 clove garlic, roughly chopped

grated zest of 1 lemon

100ml/3½ fl oz extra virgin olive oil

flaked sea salt and freshly ground
   black pepper

Time taken 20 minutes / **Serves** 4

First, make the pesto. Simply place all of the ingredients apart from the olive oil into a food processor, season with salt and pepper, and pulse until finely chopped. Slowly add the olive oil and blend until smooth. Add extra oil or a splash of water to loosen if necessary. If you're not using this straight away, cover the surface with a layer of oil to prevent discolouration.

Heat a griddle pan over a high heat. Cut the peaches into quarters and remove the stone. Rub all over with a little oil and season with salt and pepper. Lay the quarters on the griddle, cut side down, and cook for a minute or so until you have charred lines. Turn and cook the other side until charred.

Transfer to plates. Tear the burrata into chunky pieces and sit alongside the peaches. Drizzle or spoon over the pesto. Finish with a final drizzle of olive oil and twist of pepper.

Flexible
Try some cured Parma or Serrano ham with this dish.
A match made in heaven.

Seeded wasabi tofu

with pea, edamame and radish salad

Tofu is a brilliant blank canvas for adding flavour to, and the firm variety holds really well when fried. Here I've coated it in fiery wasabi paste and sesame seeds before cooking it until crunchy, yet still soft in the middle. This delicate Japanese-inspired salad is simply delicious and works brilliantly with tofu.

450g/1 lb firm silken tofu

2 tsp wasabi paste

3 tbsp sesame seeds

½ tsp salt

1 tbsp cornflour

vegetable oil, for frying

For the salad

100g/3½ oz frozen peas, defrosted

100g/3½ oz frozen podded edamame
   beans, defrosted

150g/5½ oz radishes, sliced or quartered

10g/¼ oz sliced pickled ginger, cut into strips

1 tbsp toasted sesame oil

1 tbsp groundnut oil

juice of 1 lime

2 tsp soy sauce

1 tsp honey

Time taken 20 minutes / **Serves** 4

First, make the salad. Put the peas, edamame, radishes and ginger in a mixing bowl. In a separate bowl, thoroughly mix together the sesame oil, groundnut oil, lime juice, soy sauce and honey, then pour over the salad. Toss to combine.

Drain the tofu and cut into eight slices about 1cm/½ inch thick. Pat dry on kitchen paper, then spread a little wasabi paste on one side of each slice.

Mix the sesame seeds, salt and cornflour together on a plate. Press the wasabi-coated tofu slices into the seeds until evenly coated all over.

Heat a little oil in a frying pan over a medium–low heat. Cook the tofu slices for 2–3 minutes on each side until golden.

Serve straight away with the salad.

Flexible

You can coat and pan fry steak in the same way as the tofu. Simply coat the same quantity of frying, minute or sandwich steak in the wasabi and seed mix and cook as per the method above. Leave to rest for a minute or so before slicing into pieces and serving with the salad.

Fig and goat's cheese salad
with candied walnut and orange

Sometimes simple is best and that's the rule I've followed here. There's a lovely contrast of flavours and textures coming from the luscious, juicy figs, tangy oranges, creamy goat's cheese and sweet, crunchy walnuts. These are all brought together by the piquant, zesty dressing.

100g/3½ oz walnut halves

3 tbsp caster (superfine) sugar

1 tbsp butter

1 large orange

6–10 ripe figs, depending on
   their size, quartered

200g/7 oz goat's cheese

For the dressing

2 tbsp walnut oil

2 tbsp olive oil

grated zest of ½ orange

2 tbsp white wine vinegar

1 tbsp runny honey

1 tsp Dijon mustard

flaked sea salt and freshly ground
   black pepper

Time taken 25 minutes / **Serves** 4

First of all, make the dressing. Place all of the ingredients in a small, clean jar, season with salt and pepper, and shake well until combined. Alternatively, whisk together in a small bowl.

Heat a frying pan over a medium heat. Add the walnuts, sugar and butter. Toss around until the butter and sugar melt and start to caramelise, coating the walnuts. Remove from the heat and tip onto baking parchment to cool.

Slice the top and bottom off the orange and sit on a board. Following the curve of the orange, cut away the peel and pith using a sharp knife. Cut the individual segments out of the membrane, by angling the knife towards the centre of the orange.

Scatter the figs and oranges onto one large or four small plates. Crumble the goat's cheese on top and scatter with the candied walnuts. Drizzle with the dressing and serve.

Flexible
You can buy pre-smoked duck breast, which is great added to this salad. Alternatively, you can pan fry a couple of duck breasts. Simply add a trickle of oil to a hot pan, season the duck breasts, and add skin-side down. Fry over a medium heat for 8–10 minutes, allowing the skin to release the fat while turning golden brown. Turn the breasts over and finish in a preheated oven set to 220°C/425°F/gas 7 for 7–8 minutes. Sit on a board and leave to rest for a few minutes, before slicing and serving with the salad.

Fried chickpeas, tomato and labneh flatbread

Super quick, full of flavour and good for you – what's not to love about this recipe? If you fancy making your own labneh (yoghurt cheese), try the recipe on p153, which is really easy. If you're short on time (it does require overnight preparation), then many supermarkets or Middle Eastern shops sell labneh. Greek yoghurt or some types of hummus are also great alternatives.

---

2 tbsp extra virgin olive oil, plus extra
    for drizzling
1 clove garlic, peeled and crushed
½ tsp cumin seeds
pinch dried chilli flakes
400g/14 oz tin chickpeas, drained
2 really ripe tomatoes, cut into small chunks
2 flatbreads, or tortilla bread
handful pitted black olives
handful radishes, quartered
¼ cucumber, cut into small chunks
handful mint, roughly chopped
large spoonful Labneh (p153), Greek
    yoghurt or hummus
drizzle of pomegranate molasses
flaked sea salt and freshly ground
    black pepper

Time taken 15 minutes / **Serves** 2

Gently heat the olive oil in a frying pan and add the garlic, cumin, chilli and chickpeas. Toss around in the pan until the chickpeas are heated through and starting to take on some colour. Stir in the tomatoes and continue to toss around until they start to soften. Season with salt and pepper.

Heat the flatbreads one at a time by holding over the gas flame until lightly charred each side, or in a hot, dry frying pan for about 1 minute each side.

Divide the chickpeas between two plates, and scatter with black olives, radishes, cucumber and mint. Spoon on some labneh, or Greek yoghurt, and drizzle both plates with some pomegranate molasses and extra virgin olive oil. Serve with the charred flatbread.

Flexible
Lamb works wonderfully with the Middle Eastern accents in this dish. Lamb neck fillet is full of flavour and ideal for fast cooking. Thinly slice or dice 300g / 10½ oz, then briefly fry the lamb in the hot pan for a few minutes before adding the spices and chickpeas. It's best served slightly pink, so take care not to overcook.

big
plates

Aromatic tea-smoked mushroom ramen

Smoking your own ingredients is great fun and very versatile. You don't have to own any fancy kit, just a wok lined with foil, as well as the round wire/steaming rack that sits inside. Otherwise a medium, heavy-based roasting tray will do the job.

These smoked mushrooms can be used in a variety of dishes such as risotto, salads and pasta, as well as this ramen – satisfying soul food at its best. It may look like a lengthy recipe, but it's really straightforward with very little effort needed.

_____

For the smoking mixture

2 star anise

1 tsp black peppercorns

1 tsp coriander (cilantro) seeds

125g/4½ oz uncooked rice

50g/1¾ oz Earl Grey tea leaves

75g/2½ oz brown sugar

For the mushrooms

4 large portabella mushrooms

4 tbsp extra virgin olive oil

2 cloves garlic, peeled and crushed

1 tsp soy sauce

For the ramen

350g/12oz dried ramen, udon or egg noodles

2 tsp sriracha sauce (hot chilli sauce)

1½ litres/2½ pints/6 cups hot vegetable stock

100g/3½ oz beansprouts

1 red onion, finely sliced

4 spring onions (scallions), finely sliced

2 red chillies, finely sliced

bunch coriander

1 lime, cut into wedges

flaked sea salt

Time taken 35 minutes / **Serves** 4

To prepare the smoking mixture, lightly crush the star anise, peppercorns and coriander seeds in a pestle and mortar. Mix with the rice, tea leaves and sugar. Line a wok with a layer of foil and place the smoking mixture in the centre. Sit a round wire 'steaming' rack in the middle of the wok to check it doesn't touch the smoking mixture, then remove for now.

Remove the stems from the mushrooms and cut each mushroom into 3–4 thick slices. Mix together the olive oil, garlic and soy sauce, and rub or brush all over the mushrooms. Arrange the slices on the wire rack.

Place the wok over a medium heat and when smoke starts to rise, sit the wire rack inside. Cover with a lid, and for extra security/to prevent too much smoke escaping, a tight fitting layer of aluminium foil. Reduce the heat to medium–low and cook/smoke for 20 minutes.

While the mushrooms are smoking, cook the noodles according to the pack, drain and divide between four deep bowls. Mix the sriracha sauce into the hot stock. Have a taste and add salt accordingly. Pour over the noodles, while stirring.

Arrange the smoked mushrooms over the top of the noodles and add the beansprouts, red onion, spring onion and chillies. Garnish with sprigs of coriander and lime wedges.

Flexible

Have a go at smoking alternative ingredients using this method such as peeled prawns, sliced chicken breast, fillets of fish or sliced tofu. Each of these takes roughly 20 minutes to smoke.

Southern mac 'n' cheese
with frizzled leeks

I've made numerous versions of macaroni 'n' cheese over the years, all of which hit the spot when indulgent comfort food is called for. However, I've now struck upon my all-time favourite with real Southern soul. I've used a blend of cheeses for ultimate flavour and texture: Monterey Jack for smooth, creamy texture, smoked cheddar for smokiness and nuttiness, and extra mature cheddar for sharp bite. Once the cheese sauce is mixed with the pasta, it's topped with a crisp herb crumb. Very tasty. Of course, you can just stop there and dive straight in, but I like to add a pile of crunchy shredded leeks on top, which really is the icing on the cake.

350g/12 oz dried macaroni or short pasta

70g/2½ oz butter

2 cloves garlic, peeled and crushed

50g/1¾ oz plain (all purpose) flour

600ml/21 fl oz/2½ cups full-fat milk

100g/3½ oz Monterey Jack cheese, grated

100g/3½ oz smoked cheddar cheese, grated

100g/3½ oz extra mature cheddar, grated

50g/1¾ oz panko breadcrumbs

1 tsp chopped fresh oregano, or ½ tsp dried

flaked sea salt and freshly ground
    black pepper

For the leeks

1 medium leek

2 tbsp plain (all purpose) flour

1 tsp paprika

sunflower oil, for deep frying

Time taken 45 minutes / **Serves** 4

Heat the oven to 200°C/400°F/gas 6.

Cook the pasta in boiling, salted water for 2 minutes less than the pack states, so it is slightly undercooked.

Meanwhile, melt 50g/1¾ oz of the butter in a medium–large saucepan. Add the garlic, cook for 30 seconds, then stir in the flour. Cook for a further minute, then gradually whisk in the milk until you have a smooth sauce. Allow to simmer for 5 minutes, stirring continuously until thickened.

Remove the pan from the heat and stir in the cheeses and drained pasta. Season with salt and pepper and transfer to one large ovenproof dish, or individual dishes.

Melt the remaining 20g/¾ oz of butter, then toss with the breadcrumbs and oregano. Scatter over the top of the macaroni cheese and bake in the oven for about 20 minutes until crisp and golden.

While the mac 'n' cheese is in the oven, cut the leek in half across the middle, then finely slice each piece into thin strips the thickness of a matchstick. Rinse to wash away any soil or grit then shake off any excess water and pat dry with kitchen paper. Put in a bowl and toss well with the flour and paprika.

Heat about 5cm/2 inches of oil in a wok or medium saucepan until it starts to shimmer. Working in batches, fry the leeks for about 30 seconds until light golden. Drain on kitchen paper and sprinkle with salt.

When the macaroni cheese is baked, serve with the frizzled leeks piled on top or on the side.

Flexible
For a meat twist to individual portions, bake the mac 'n' cheese in individual dishes. Line the inside edge of some dishes with Parma or Serrano ham, leaving it to loosely hang over the edges. Fill the dishes with the mac 'n' cheese and scatter with crumbs before baking as per the recipe.

Creamy mushroom, leek and chestnut pie

The combination of mushrooms, leeks, chestnuts and thyme are bound together in a silky smooth sauce using fortified Madeira wine, porcini mushroom stock and my wildcard… tofu. Not only does the tofu keep the fat content lower than if you used cream, it also gives a big hit of protein too.

20g/¾ oz dried porcini mushrooms

300g/10½ oz silken tofu

40g/1½ oz butter

2 tbsp olive oil

250g/7 oz chestnut mushrooms, halved

250g/7 oz portabella mushrooms, thickly sliced

2 large leeks, sliced

4 cloves garlic, peeled and crushed

200g/7 oz ready-to-eat chestnuts,
    roughly chopped

approx. 2 tsp fresh thyme leaves

2 tbsp cornflour

80ml/2½ fl oz/1/3 cup Madeira wine

2 tsp sherry vinegar

375g/13 oz all-butter puff pastry block

flour, for dusting

1 egg yolk mixed with 1 tbsp milk (egg wash)

pinch poppy seeds (optional)

flaked sea salt and freshly ground
    black pepper

Time taken 1 hour 15 minutes + 30 minutes soaking / **Serves** 4

Heat the oven to 200°C/400°F/gas 6.

Place the porcini mushrooms in 400ml/14 fl oz/1⅔ cups of boiling water and leave to soak for 30 minutes. Drain and reserve the liquid.

Put the tofu and reserved porcini liquid into a blender or food processor and blitz until completely smooth and creamy. Set aside.

Melt half of the butter with 1 tablespoon of the olive oil in a large saucepan over a high heat and fry the chestnut mushrooms and portabella mushrooms until they have browned and softened. Remove from the pan. Reduce the heat to medium–low, add the remaining butter and sauté the leeks for a few minutes until softened and just starting to colour.

Stir in the porcini mushrooms, fried mushrooms, garlic, chestnuts and thyme. Cook for about 1 minute. Mix the cornflour into the Madeira wine to make a loose paste, then add to the pan along with the tofu and porcini 'cream'. Bring to a gentle simmer and cook for 3–4 minutes for the sauce to thicken. Stir in the vinegar and season with salt and pepper. Transfer to a pie dish or individual dishes and leave to cool slightly.

Roll the pastry out on a lightly floured surface until just a little bigger than the dish/dishes. Brush a little egg wash over the rim of the dish/dishes and sit the pastry on top, pressing the edges to seal. Brush the top with the egg wash and scatter with poppy seeds (if using). Pierce a hole in the centre to allow steam to escape when cooking and sit on a baking tray.

Bake in the oven for 30 minutes or until the pastry is puffed up and nicely golden. Rest for 5–10 minutes before serving.

Flexible
This is too good to mess with really, but if you have leftover roast chicken, turkey or diced ham you want to use up, reduce the mushroom quantity accordingly and stir the cooked meat through the sauce at the end.

Spiced tofu poke

Poke (poh-keh) bowls started to emerge around the 1970s in Hawaii when fishermen would use raw fish and cooked rice to create a sort of deconstructed sushi. It has become hugely popular due to its versatility, ranging from healthy to indulgent. Variations now include different bases, such as brown rice or courgette noodles, and you can top with all sorts of proteins including sushi-grade cubes of tuna or salmon, cooked chicken, crab, tofu, and numerous salad ingredients.

150g/5½ oz Thai jasmine rice

2 tbsp rice vinegar

1 tsp sesame oil

1 tbsp mirin

2 tbsp soy sauce

pinch dried chilli flakes

juice of 1 lime

1 tsp toasted black or white sesame seeds,
    plus more to serve

200g/7 oz firm silken tofu, cut into small cubes

¼ cucumber, finely sliced

1 avocado, stoned and cubed

2 spring onions (scallions), finely sliced

1 sheet nori, snipped into shards

flaked sea salt

Time taken 45 minutes / **Serves** 2

Put the rice in a saucepan with a pinch of salt and 200ml/7 fl oz/ scant 1 cup of water. Bring to the boil, cover with a lid and cook on low for 10 minutes without removing the lid. Remove the pan from the heat, and leave the lid on for a further 5 minutes. Tip onto a tray or plate, sprinkle with the rice vinegar and leave to cool.

Mix together the sesame oil, mirin, soy sauce, chilli flakes, lime juice and sesame seeds in a large bowl. Add the tofu and cucumber, and toss in the dressing. Leave to marinate for about 30 minutes.

Gently fold the avocado into the tofu bowl. Divide the rice between two bowls and top with the tofu mix. Scatter with the spring onion, more sesame seeds, nori and any dressing left in the bowl.

Flexible
Rather than using tofu, swap for the same quantity of a more authentic poke ingredient: raw tuna or salmon. The key is to use the best quality fish you can get and dice it into bite-size pieces. Marinate it as you would the tofu and serve as above.

Maple butter cornbread

Paired with a spicy chilli dish (opposite), the buttery sweetness of this bread takes the edge off the heat. The only problem is you'll keep going back for more! (Picture on following page.)

200g/7 oz cornmeal or fine polenta

150g/5½ oz plain (all purpose) flour

2 tsp bicarbonate of soda (baking soda)

1½ tsp onion salt

1 egg

300ml/10 fl oz/1¼ cups buttermilk

175ml/6 fl oz/cup milk

75g/2½ oz butter, plus an extra knob

75ml/2½ fl oz/⅓ cup maple syrup

Time taken 25 minutes / **Serves** 8

Heat the oven to 200°C/400°F/gas 6.

Place the cornmeal or polenta in a large bowl with the flour, bicarbonate of soda and onion salt.

Break the egg into a jug and mix with the buttermilk and milk. Pour into the dry ingredients then mix until just combined, making sure you don't overmix otherwise you will make the cornbread tough.

Place a 23cm–25cm/9–10 inch non-stick ovenproof frying pan/skillet over a high heat and add the knob of butter. Swirl around to coat the inside of the pan. Pour in the bread batter and level the surface. Transfer to the oven and cook for 15 minutes, until golden and just firm.

While the cornbread is cooking, melt together the measured butter and the maple syrup to give you a golden, sweet liquid.

As soon as the cornbread is cooked, immediately pour over the maple butter, covering the whole surface. Return to the oven for 1 minute allowing the maple butter to bubble around the edges of the pan.

Remove from the heat and serve hot, cut into wedges or simply spooned straight out of the pan.

Flexible

Fry 150g/5½ oz diced smoked pancetta or smoked streaky bacon until golden, then add the butter and maple syrup as per the method above. Pour over the cornbread and return to the oven for 1 minute as above.

Black bean chilli and DIY guacamole

Thick, rich, hearty, spicy and smoky –
what's not to like? This recipe makes
a large quantity that is perfect for
sharing with a group of friends.
Put the big pot in the middle of
the table and arrange your own
guacamole components around it.
Maple Butter Cornbread (opposite)
is an ideal accompaniment.
(Picture on following page.)

---

3 tbsp olive oil

2 large onions, finely chopped

6 cloves garlic, crushed

2 tsp cumin seeds, lightly crushed

2 star anise

1 cinnamon stick, broken in half

250ml/9 fl oz/1 cup red wine

4 x 400g/14 oz tins black beans, drained

2 x 400g/14 oz tins chopped tomatoes

2 tbsp tomato purée

3 whole roasted red (bell) peppers, from a jar,
   finely chopped

2½ tbsp chipotle paste

2 tbsp cocoa powder

pinch dried chilli flakes (optional)

flaked sea salt and freshly ground
   black pepper

For the DIY guacamole

250ml/9 fl oz/1 cup sour cream

2 tsp paprika

bunch coriander (cilantro), finely shredded

1 red onion, finely sliced

1 green chilli, finely sliced

3 ripe avocados, peeled, stone removed
   and sliced

2 limes, cut into wedges

Time taken 1 hour / **Serves** 6–8

Heat the oil in a large casserole or saucepan. Add the onion, garlic, cumin seeds, star anise and cinnamon stick, and gently sauté for around 10 minutes until the onion is softened and becoming nicely golden.

Increase the heat and add the red wine. Boil for 1 minute to reduce, then add the black beans, tomatoes, tomato purée, red peppers, chipotle paste and cocoa powder, and season with salt and pepper. If you know you want a really spicy chilli, add a pinch of chilli flakes. You can also add this nearer to the end of the cooking time after you've had a taste.

Bring to the simmer, cover with a lid and cook on a low heat for 35–45 minutes, stirring every so often, until rich and thickened.

While the chilli is cooking, mix together the sour cream and paprika. Place in a serving bowl and put the other guacamole components into their own individual serving bowls, popping them all in the middle of the table. When you serve the chilli, everyone can knock together their own guacamole and mop up the chilli juices with a wedge of cornbread.

Flexible
If you're missing the meat in your chilli, you can easily
switch the black beans for 1kg/2 lb 4 oz beef or pork
mince (or a mix of the two). Add to the pan after you've
sautéed the onion, garlic and spices. Fry over a high
heat until the mince has browned. Add the red wine and
continue as above. You can also add 1 tin of black or
kidney beans after the red wine if you'd like a mix.

Pearl barley and sweet potato stew
with radish and spring onion salsa

This is a light, summery stew with a crunchy, tangy salsa over the top that's packed with fresh flavours. I like to serve it with spoonfuls of Labneh (p153) for some added protein. It's really easy to make your own or you can buy it from large supermarkets or Middle Eastern shops. As an alternative, you can crumble some feta cheese over the top.

----

2 tbsp olive oil

1 onion, chopped

2 cloves garlic, peeled and crushed

2 tsp cumin seeds

1 tsp hot smoked paprika

275g/9¾ oz pearl barley

750ml/26 fl oz/3 cups hot vegetable stock

approx. 650g/1 lb 7 oz (2 medium–large
    sweet potatoes), peeled

1 tbsp tomato purée

200g/7 oz labneh or feta cheese

flaked sea salt and freshly ground
    black pepper

For the salsa

75g/2½ oz radishes, finely sliced

5 spring onions (scallions), chopped

3 tomatoes, deseeded and chopped

juice of 1 lime

small handful coriander (cilantro), chopped

2 tbsp extra virgin olive oil

Time taken 45 minutes / **Serves** 4

Heat the olive oil in a deep-sided pan and gently sauté the onion, garlic, cumin seeds and paprika for 8–10 minutes until sticky and golden. Add the pearl barley and stir around in the pan for about 30 seconds before adding the stock. Cover with a lid and simmer for 10 minutes.

Cut the sweet potato into 2–3cm/¾–1¼ inch chunks and add to the pan with the tomato purée. Cover and cook for around 15 minutes until the sweet potato is completely cooked through. Season with salt and pepper. If the stew seems too dry, add some extra stock.

While the stew is cooking, mix together all of the salsa ingredients, and season with salt and pepper.

Serve the cooked stew with the salsa spooned on top, sprinkled with nuggets of labneh or crumbled feta cheese.

Flexible
Add around 100g / 3½ oz diced chorizo to the pan with the onions to get a much deeper smoky flavour and give a rich red colour to the stew.

Bulgar wheat pilaf
with grilled nectarines and tzatziki

When in season, nectarines or peaches are both delicious served on top of this aromatic pilaf. I'll often make the pilaf at other times of the year, just to remind me of those lovely summer days, so I swap the nectarines for other seasonal fruits such as figs or plums.

There's also a lovely recipe for tzatziki here, which is best made ahead of time to give the flavours a chance to infuse.

---

2 tbsp olive oil, plus extra for drizzling

2 large onions, finely sliced

4 cloves garlic, peeled and crushed

1 bay leaf

½ tsp ground cinnamon

200g/7 oz bulgar wheat

400ml/14 fl oz/1⅔ cups vegetable stock

4 nectarines (not too ripe)

½ tsp cayenne pepper

small bunch parsley, roughly chopped

100g/3½ oz feta cheese

75g/2½ oz pistachio nuts

flaked sea salt

For the tzatziki

¼ cucumber, peeled, halved and seeds removed

1 tsp flaked sea salt

1 small clove garlic, crushed

1 tsp red wine vinegar

1 tbsp finely chopped mint

100g/3½ oz Greek yoghurt

Time taken 50 minutes / **Serves** 4

To make the tzatziki, finely chop or grate the cucumber, place in a sieve and sprinkle with the sea salt. Leave to drain for around 10 minutes before squeezing out the excess water. Mix with the garlic, vinegar, mint and yoghurt. Season to taste and keep chilled until needed.

Heat the oven to 200°C/400°F/gas 6.

Heat 1 tablespoon of the olive oil in a large saucepan and gently cook the onions for about 10 minutes until golden brown. Add the garlic, bay leaf and cinnamon. Continue to cook for a further 5 minutes.

Stir in the bulgar wheat and stock, and bring to a simmer. Cover with a lid and cook over a low heat for 10 minutes. Remove from the heat, set aside and keep covered to allow the stock to be absorbed for a further 10 minutes.

While you are cooking the bulgar wheat, heat a griddle pan over a high heat. Cut each nectarine in quarters and remove the stones. Drizzle each quarter with olive oil and season with salt and the cayenne pepper. Sit the fruit cut-side down on the hot griddle for about 1 minute, until you have dark griddle lines. Carefully lift off the pan with a palette knife and sit the fruit in a roasting tray. Bake in the oven for 15 minutes until tender.

Run a fork through the bulgar wheat and add the parsley. Toss around, then serve topped with the nectarines. Scatter the feta and pistachios over the top, and add a good dollop of tzatziki.

Flexible
You can add either meat or fish to this recipe, depending on taste. Try slicing 400g / 14 oz monkfish fillet into medallions and griddle for 5–6 minutes, turning halfway. Serve with the griddled nectarines. For a more economical weeknight meal, cut 4 boneless lamb steaks into thick slices, rub in olive oil, season with salt, a pinch of cayenne pepper and ½ tsp each of ground cinnamon and coriander. Griddle for 5–6 minutes, turning halfway. Rest for a couple of minutes before serving either with or without the nectarines.

Seasonal vegetable tarts

This is such a handy recipe for any time of the year. You start with the same creamy ricotta cheese base spread on to puff pastry, then mix and match your toppings depending on what's in season or whatever you fancy using.

You can make one large tart, but I quite like to make these as individual tarts as you have the option of customising them by adding meat or fish.

---

1 sheet ready rolled puff pastry, approx. 350g/12 oz

250g/9 oz ricotta cheese

2 eggs, lightly beaten

50g/1¾ oz grated parmesan cheese or vegetarian equivalent

1 clove garlic, peeled and crushed

olive oil, for drizzling

flaked sea salt and freshly ground black pepper

Seasonal suggestions

Summer = 450g/1 lb quartered tomatoes, 1 sliced courgette (zucchini), and 1 handful torn basil

Autumn = 1 medium butternut squash, cut into wedges, tossed in oil and roasted until tender, 1 tbsp chopped sage and 1 handful toasted pinenuts

Winter = 350g/12 oz cooked beetroot wedges, 1 tsp chopped thyme and 1 large handful chopped walnuts

Spring = 250g/9 oz asparagus tips, 1 handful chopped mint and 150g/5½ oz defrosted peas

Time taken 40 minutes / **Serves** 4

Heat the oven to 200°C/400°F/gas 6.

Unroll the pastry and sit on a non-stick baking sheet. If you are making this as individual tarts, cut into 4 rectangles and sit slightly spaced apart. Prick the surface of the pastry several times with a fork.

Mix together the ricotta, eggs, parmesan, garlic, seasoning and chopped herb of your choice from the seasonal selection. Spread over the pastry base/bases leaving a border around 1cm/½ inch thick.

Arrange your chosen toppings on top of the ricotta mixture, pressing down lightly. Drizzle over some olive oil and season with salt and pepper. Bake in the oven for about 30 minutes for a large tart, or 20 minutes for individual tarts, until the ricotta mixture is just set and becoming golden.

Remove from the oven and serve hot or cool.

Flexible

Add 250g/9 oz warm flaked smoked salmon, smoked trout or smoked mackerel to the top of the tarts before baking. Or try adding around 100g/3½ oz cured meats just before serving, such as Parma ham, Serrano ham, chorizo or salami (these are particularly good with the summer, autumn and spring toppings). Or 100g/3½ oz sliced smoked duck or chicken would work well with the winter topping suggestion.

Tray-baked summer vegetables
with chilli and borlotti beans

This is a great store cupboard saviour, and something you can whip up when you think you have nothing in for dinner. It's perfect as a well-balanced main course for two, or you can serve it alongside a roast chicken (p173) and some lemony couscous when cooking for meat eaters.

---

1 large red onion, peeled and cut into wedges

1 fennel, cut into slim wedges

1 large courgette (zucchini), cut into 1cm/½ inch thick slices

1 red or green chilli, halved and deseeded

4 bay leaves

olive oil

3 ripe tomatoes, quartered

400g/14 oz tin borlotti beans, drained

large handful pitted black olives

80ml/2½ fl oz/⅓ cup white wine

flaked sea salt and freshly ground black pepper

Time taken 50 minutes / **Serves** 2

Heat the oven to 220°C/425°F/gas 7.

Put the onion, fennel, courgette, chilli and bay leaves into a roasting tray, making sure it's large enough so the veg aren't too squashed together. Add a really good glug of olive oil, season with salt and pepper, and toss together.

Put in the oven for 20 minutes, turning the vegetables once or twice, until they are softening and starting to colour. Add the tomatoes and continue to cook for a further 10 minutes.

Add the beans, olives and white wine. Continue to cook for a further 5 minutes, until the tomatoes are still holding their shape but you have bubbling juices in the pan.

Serve hot straight from the oven, or you can also serve this when cooled to room temperature.

Flexible

I really like to add sea bass in this tray bake, as it has a lovely texture and flavour and doesn't take long to cook. Once the veggies have had the first 20 minutes of cooking time, sit two sea bass fillets (seasoned and rubbed with olive oil) on top. Scatter the tomatoes around the edges. Return to the oven and continue as above, giving the fish a total of 15 minutes cooking time. Alternatively, add 100g/3½ oz diced chorizo into the pan with the veggies. The rich red oils and smoky flavour works really well with the other ingredients.

Sweet potato fries

You'll need a side or two to serve with the Ultimate Veggie Burgers (opposite), and you can't beat these crisp sweet potato fries and crunchy, creamy, tangy homemade coleslaw. (Picture on following page.)

---

4 medium–large sweet potatoes

1½ tbsp fine polenta

½ tsp paprika

olive oil

flaked sea salt and freshly ground
  black pepper

Time taken 40–45 minutes / **Serves** 4

Heat the oven to 220°C/425°F/gas 7.

Peel the potatoes and cut into long 1cm/½ inch chip shapes. Wash well in cold water and pat dry. Tip onto a baking tray. Scatter over the polenta, paprika, pinch of salt, pepper and a decent drizzle of olive oil (enough to lightly coat the potatoes). Toss together and bake in the oven for 30–40 minutes, turning a few times throughout, until golden and crispy.

Fennel and radish coleslaw

---

1 red-skinned apple, such as Braeburn
  or Pink Lady

1 tbsp lemon juice

½ fennel

¼ red cabbage

125g/4½ oz radishes

2 shallots, peeled

125g/4½ oz crème fraîche

50g/2 oz natural (plain) yoghurt

2 tsp Dijon mustard

2 tsp cider vinegar

1 tsp celery salt

flaked sea salt and freshly ground
  black pepper

Time taken 15 minutes / **Serves** 6–8

Remove the core from the apple and cut the apple into matchstick size pieces. Put into a large bowl and toss in the lemon juice.

Very finely slice or shred the fennel, cabbage, radishes and shallots either using a very sharp knife and steady hand, a mandolin or a slicer blade on a food processor. Add to the apple and toss everything together.

Mix together the crème fraîche, yoghurt, Dijon mustard, cider vinegar and celery salt. Season with a good twist of pepper and mix thoroughly into the vegetables. Season to taste.

Chill in the fridge for about 1 hour for the dressing to absorb into the vegetables a little and all of the flavours to combine.

Ultimate veggie burgers
with onion marmalade and harissa mayo

Quite often a veggie burger is thought of as a healthy option, but this is an indulgent 'dirty' burger! It's topped with melting smoked cheese and stacked into a soft brioche bun with sticky sweet onions, spiced mayo, gherkins and some lettuce. For the ultimate experience, serve with some Sweet Potato Fries and Fennel and Radish Coleslaw (opposite). (Picture on following page.)

For the burger
olive oil

250–300g/9–10½ oz flat or portabella
    mushrooms, cut into approx. 1cm/½
      inch pieces

1 large (approx. 400g/14 oz) aubergine
    (eggplant), cut into approx. 1cm/½
      inch pieces

6 cloves garlic, peeled and crushed

3 tbsp brown sauce (such as HP or Daddies)

175g/6 oz fresh breadcrumbs

1 egg

1½ tsp mixed dried herbs

sea salt and freshly ground black pepper

For the onion marmalade
25g/10 oz butter

3 red onions, thinly sliced

1 clove garlic, peeled and crushed

60ml/2 fl oz balsamic vinegar

2 tbsp soft dark brown sugar

To serve
4 brioche buns, split in half

100g/3½ oz sliced smoked cheddar cheese

6 tbsp mayonnaise

1–2 tsp harissa paste

baby gem lettuce leaves

sliced gherkins

Time taken 1 hour + 1 hour chilling / **Serves** 4

To make the marmalade, melt the butter in a large saucepan. Add the sliced onions and garlic, and season well. Gently cook over a low–medium heat until the onions are deep golden and caramelised, around 20 minutes. Increase the heat and add the balsamic vinegar to deglaze the pan. Add the sugar and cook for a further 5 minutes, then season again. Cool to room temperature.

To make the burgers, heat 2 tablespoons of olive oil in a large frying pan and fry the mushrooms over a high heat until coloured and any moisture has cooked away. Tip into a bowl to cool. Return the pan to the heat. Heat a further 2 tablespoons of oil and fry the aubergine until golden and tender, tossing around in the pan, to prevent it from burning. Remove from the heat and also leave to cool.

Put the cooled mushrooms and aubergine into a food processor along with the garlic, brown sauce, breadcrumbs, egg and herbs. Season with salt and pepper and blend until the mixture is thoroughly mixed. Using wet hands, firmly shape into four thick burgers and put on a parchment-lined tray or plate. Chill in the fridge for 1 hour.

Heat a glug of olive oil in a frying pan. Fry the burgers over a medium–high heat for around 4 minutes each side until cooked.

Heat the grill to medium–high. Halve the brioche buns and lightly toast the cut sides. At the same time, top the burgers with slices of cheese and sit under the grill until melted. Mix the mayonnaise and harissa together. Spread some onto the bottom halves of the buns, then lay on some lettuce and a spoon of onion marmalade. Sit the burger on top, add sliced gherkins and finally a dollop of harissa mayonnaise. Lightly press down with the bun lid.

Flexible
For a more traditional meat burger, sauté 1 chopped onion and 2 cloves of garlic in 25g / 1 oz butter. Leave to cool then mix with 600g / 1 lb 5 oz good-quality minced steak, 6 rashers of finely diced smoked streaky bacon, 1 beaten egg, 1 teaspoon of Dijon mustard and plenty of salt and pepper. Shape into four burgers and chill for 30 minutes. Fry in a trickle of olive oil for 3–4 minutes each side (medium) before finishing with the cheese on top under the grill.

Aubergine and quinoa 'meatballs'
with tomato sauce

These look and (almost) taste like traditional meatballs – they will surprise anyone who eats them when they realise they are completely meat free. I like to serve these with a homemade tomato pasta sauce, plenty of spaghetti and shavings of parmesan, but they also work as a canapé (skewered with a cocktail stick and with a tomato sauce to dip into), or wrapped in flatbread with salad and garlic mayo.

100g/3½ oz quinoa

olive oil

1 onion, finely chopped

2 cloves garlic, peeled and crushed

2 medium–large aubergines (eggplants)
(approx. 650g/1 lb 7 oz), chopped into small
dice (approx. 5mm/¼ inch)

75g/2½ oz breadcrumbs

50g/1¾ oz parmesan cheese or vegetarian
equivalent, plus extra to serve

50g/1¾ oz pitted black olives, finely chopped

1 egg, lightly beaten

4 tbsp chia seeds

small handful basil leaves

cooked spaghetti or other pasta, to serve

flaked sea salt and freshly ground
black pepper

For the sauce

2 x 400g/14 oz tins chopped tomatoes

185ml/6 fl oz/¾ cup red wine

2 cloves garlic, peeled and crushed

2 tbsp olive oil

1 tsp balsamic vinegar

1 tsp caster (superfine) sugar

Time taken 1 hour + about 1 hour chilling / **Serves** 6

To cook the quinoa, heat a medium saucepan over a high heat. Add the quinoa and shake around in the pan for about 30 seconds to start to toast it. Pour in 250ml/9 fl oz/1 cup of water and allow to boil for 1 minute. Reduce the heat to low. Cover with a lid and leave to cook for 10 minutes. After this time, turn off the heat and leave for 5 minutes before taking off the lid and running a fork through the quinoa to separate the grains.

Heat a glug of oil in a large frying pan over a medium heat. Add the onion and sauté for 5 minutes until it is starting to soften but not colour. Add the garlic and aubergine. Sauté for about 10–12 minutes until the aubergine is completely softened. Remove from the heat, transfer to a large bowl and leave to cool for about 10 minutes.

Put the aubergine and onion mixture, quinoa, breadcrumbs, parmesan, olives, egg, chia seeds and basil into a food processor. Season with salt and pepper, then pulse until the mixture holds together. Firmly shape into golf ball-sized balls, making approximately 30 in total. Sit on a parchment or cling film lined tray or plate and chill in the fridge for about 1 hour.

To make the sauce, put all of the ingredients in a saucepan, season and bring to a simmer. Cook over a low heat for 20–30 minutes until the tomatoes have thickened (the time will depend on the brand of tomatoes as some are thicker than others to start with).

Heat a glug of olive oil in a large non-stick frying pan. Add the 'meatballs' and cook over a medium–high heat, gently turning/ rolling frequently, until lightly golden. You may need to do a couple of batches depending on the size of your pan.

Gently stir in the tomato sauce, spoon over cooked spaghetti and scatter with parmesan.

Flexible
The aubergine can be swapped for 500g / 1 lb 2 oz minced beef, chicken, pork or lamb. Sauté the onion and leave to cool before mixing with the raw mince and remaining meatball ingredients. Roll into balls and chill as above. Fry the meatballs as above on a medium heat for 12–15 minutes, turning as they become golden and cooked through. Pour over the sauce, heat through and serve with spaghetti.

Braised lentils and cauliflower steaks
with brazil nut gremolata

Who'd have thought the humble cauliflower could have so many uses – it's certainly come on a long way from being boiled to death and plonked on the side of a roast. It can be blitzed in a food processor to give you cauliflower couscous or cauliflower rice, coated in spices and roasted whole or in florets (such as Spicy Roast Cauliflower, p83) and even thickly sliced into steaks, which is exactly what I've done here. It's an impressive dish to serve at a dinner party.

---

4 tbsp olive oil

1 onion, finely chopped

2 cloves garlic, peeled and crushed

1 stick celery, finely chopped

2 tsp fennel seeds, lightly crushed

2 bay leaves

2 sprigs thyme

150ml/5 fl oz/⅔ cup white wine

250g/9 oz puy lentils

20g/¾ oz dried mushrooms

2 tbsp tomato purée

1 litre/1¾ pints/4 cups vegetable stock

2 medium cauliflowers

flaked sea salt and freshly ground
   black pepper

For the gremolata

75g/2½ oz brazil nuts, chopped

small bunch parsley, chopped

small bunch basil, chopped

finely grated zest and juice of ½ lemon

Time taken 1 hour 15 mins / **Serves** 4

Heat the oven to 180°C/350°F/gas 4.

Heat 2 tablespoons of olive oil in an ovenproof sauté pan or casserole dish. Add the onion, garlic, celery, fennel seeds, bay leaves and thyme. Cook for about 10 minutes over a low–medium heat until the vegetables are softened.

Increase the heat under the pan and pour in the wine. Bring to the boil and reduce by half. Stir in the lentils, dried mushrooms, tomato purée and vegetable stock. Bring to a simmer, cover with a lid and put in the oven for 30 minutes. Remove the lid and continue to cook for a further 20 minutes.

While the lentils are cooking, remove the leaves from the cauliflowers and cut two 'steaks' about 1–2cm/½–¾ inch thick through the thickest part of each cauliflower. (The outer edges that will break up can be used for other recipes such as Cauliflower Cream Cheese Soup, p41.)

Heat 1 tablespoon of olive oil in a large frying pan. Fry the steaks for around 2 minutes each side until golden. You may need to do this in batches, depending on the size of your pan, adding extra oil if necessary. Transfer to a baking tray, season with salt and pepper, and bake in the oven for 15 minutes until tender.

To make the gremolata, toast the brazil nuts in the oven for 6–8 minutes until golden. Cool slightly, then mix with the herbs, lemon juice, lemon zest and season with salt and pepper.

Remove the thyme sprigs and bay leaves from the lentils and check for seasoning. Spoon onto plates and sit the steaks on top. Finish by scattering the gremolata over the top.

Flexible
A fabulous alternative to the cauliflower is to pan fry thick white fish fillets, 1 per person, such as cod, haddock, hake, pollock or coley. Add a trickle of olive oil to a pan over a medium–high heat. Dust the fish lightly in seasoned flour and pan fry skin side down for 2–3 minutes until golden. Turn over and continue to cook in the oven, alongside the lentils, for 6–8 minutes depending on the thickness of the fish.

Roast Cajun mushrooms and bean salad
with creamy cashew and lime dressing

This is a satisfying and wonderfully healthy salad that has everything covered: nutritious crunchy greens, protein and fibre. But really the best thing about this is the cashew and lime dressing – it's something you can make time and time again for other salads or even as a dip. Once made it will keep for up to 5 days in the fridge, just give it a good stir before using.

---

2 cloves garlic, peeled and crushed

1 tsp dried oregano

1 tsp paprika

pinch dried chilli flakes

1 tsp ground cumin

3 tbsp olive oil

1 tsp flaked sea salt

4 large flat mushrooms

2 large sweet potatoes, peeled and cut into
    small chunks

150g/5½ oz tenderstem broccoli, cut into
    small pieces

100g/3½ oz green beans, halved

100g/3½ oz kale leaves, torn into small pieces

2 x 400g/14 oz tins beans such as kidney,
    black eye, cannellini, haricot, borlotti or
        butter beans, drained

1 bunch spring onions (scallions), chopped

freshly ground black pepper

For the dressing

80g/2¾ oz cashew nuts

80ml/2½ fl oz /⅓ cup extra virgin olive oil

½ tsp flaked sea salt

juice of 1 lime

small bunch coriander (cilantro)

½ green chilli

Time taken 45 minutes + 2 hours soaking / **Serves** 4

To make the dressing, soak the cashew nuts in a bowl of cold water for about 2 hours. Drain well and rinse in fresh water. Tip into a blender and blitz with 5 tablespoons of cold water, the olive oil, the salt, lime juice, coriander and chilli, until smooth and creamy. Have a taste and add extra salt if needed. Keep in the fridge until needed.

Heat the oven to 220°C/425°F/gas 7. Mix together the garlic, oregano, paprika, chilli flakes, cumin, olive oil, the salt and plenty of freshly ground black pepper. Add the mushrooms and sweet potato pieces to coat in the mixture. Transfer to a roasting tray, and put in the oven for 20–25 minutes, turning a couple of times throughout for even cooking.

While the mushrooms and sweet potatoes are roasting, lightly cook the broccoli and green beans by either steaming or boiling in water for 3–4 minutes, adding the kale for the last minute. Put in a large bowl and toss together with the beans, spring onions, some salt and pepper and a couple of large spoonfuls of the dressing.

Serve the salad with the mushrooms, either left whole or sliced in half, and sweet potato sitting on top, and spoon over more dressing.

Flexible

Swap the mushrooms for 1 chunky fillet per person of white fish, such as cod, haddock, coley or pollock. Coat in the spices and cook with the sweet potato, but only turn the sweet potatoes during cooking.

Malaysian squash and courgette rendang
with red lentils

This is a regular in my house and I'll often make double the amount of curry paste and keep it in a jar in the fridge for future quick-prep suppers. The squash, red pepper and courgette provide fabulous colour, and the added split red lentils result in a thick sauce that's nutritionally balanced.

---

olive oil

8–10 cardamom pods, crushed

1 cinnamon stick

½ tsp whole cloves

3 kaffir lime leaves, torn into quarters

1 butternut squash, peeled and cut into
    3–4cm/1¼–1½ inch chunks

1 red (bell) pepper, deseeded and cut into
    2–3cm/¾–1¼ inch chunks

150g/7 oz red split lentils

400ml/14 fl oz tin coconut milk

400ml/14 fl oz/1⅔ cups vegetable stock

handful coconut flakes

1 tbsp agave or maple syrup

2 medium courgettes (zucchini), cut into
    2–3cm/ ¾–1¼ inch chunks

flaked sea salt

lime wedges, to serve

For the spice paste

4 shallots, peeled and roughly chopped

4 cloves garlic, peeled

1 stalk lemongrass, roughly chopped

2½cm/1 inch piece ginger, peeled and
    roughly chopped

2½cm/1 inch piece galangal, peeled and
    roughly chopped

1 tsp turmeric

2 long red chillies, roughly chopped

1 tbsp tamarind paste

1 tbsp sunflower or groundnut oil

1 tsp flaked sea salt

Time taken 40 minutes / **Serves** 4

To make the spice paste, put all the ingredients into a small food processor or blender and blitz to form a smooth paste. Set aside or keep covered in the fridge for up to 1 week.

Heat the oil in a wok or large frying pan. Add the paste and fry for a minute or so. Add the cardamom pods, cinnamon stick, cloves and lime leaves. Fry for a further minute, then add the butternut squash, red pepper and lentils. Stir around to coat in the paste, then pour in the coconut milk and stock. Bring to a simmer, cover with a lid and cook for 10 minutes.

Meanwhile, heat a small dry frying pan over a medium heat. Add the coconut flakes and agave/maple syrup, and toss around in the pan until golden and crisp. Remove from the heat.

Stir the courgette into the curry. Return to a simmer and continue to cook, with the lid off, for a further 10 minutes. Season with salt to taste.

Serve the curry in bowls and scatter over the coconut. Serve with lime to squeeze over.

Flexible

The spice paste can be used in the same way as above to make a chicken rendang. Swap the squash, lentils and courgette for 4 large chicken breasts (cut into chunks) and cook as above. You won't need to use the vegetable stock as this is only needed when using lentils. Reduce the simmering time to just 10 minutes in total, rather than 20 minutes. If you fancy adding a vegetable such as baby corn or green beans, then add them when the chicken is half cooked.

Smoky roots and brazil nut crumble

I grew up eating lots of hearty stews, pies and savoury crumbles. Most of these were meat based, but there was one vegetarian dish my mum would make that was packed with all the odds and ends in the fridge, mixed with a cheese sauce and topped with a buttery crumble. I've given her recipe a modern makeover, creating a lighter sauce and giving the crumble a cheesy, nutty crunch. My kids love it.

For the filling

1kg/2 lb 4 oz root vegetables, such as parsnip, swede, celeriac, carrot, sweet potato or squash, peeled and cut into 3cm/1¼ inch chunks

2 onions, peeled and cut into wedges

few sprigs of rosemary

2 tsp sweet smoked paprika

olive oil

200ml/7 fl oz/scant 1 cup crème fraîche

3 tbsp cornflour

1 tbsp wholegrain mustard

185ml/6 fl oz/¾ cup white wine

600ml/21 fl oz/2½ cups vegetable stock

flaked sea salt and freshly ground black pepper

For the topping

75g/2½ oz butter

1 clove garlic, peeled and crushed

75g/2½ oz plain (all purpose) flour

50g/1¾ oz oats

75g/2½ oz brazil nuts, chopped into small pieces

50g/1¾ oz grated parmesan cheese (or vegetarian equivalent) or cheddar cheese

Time taken 1½–1¾ hours / **Serves** 4–6

Heat the oven to 200°C/400°F/gas 6.

Put the root vegetables, onions, rosemary and smoked paprika in a roasting tray and toss in a glug of olive oil. Season with salt and pepper, then roast in the oven for 35–45 minutes, turning a few times, until the vegetables are completely tender and starting to become golden.

While the vegetables are roasting, beat together the crème fraîche, cornflour and mustard and set aside.

For the crumble topping, lightly run together the butter, garlic, flour and oats. Season and stir in the brazil nuts and cheese.

Remove the vegetables from the oven and sit the tray over a gentle heat on the hob. Pour in the white wine and bring to the boil. Cook for 30 seconds before adding the stock. Bring to the boil, then stir in the crème fraîche mixture, until thickened slightly. Remove the rosemary sprigs and season to taste.

Spoon into one large or small individual ovenproof dishes. Scatter the crumble over the top, then return to the oven for around 30 minutes until the top is golden and the filling is bubbling.

Flexible
You can transform this into a chicken and vegetable crumble. Cut down on the root vegetables by one-third and add around 500g / 1 lb 2 oz chicken thighs to the roasting tray. Once roasted together, the recipe can be followed as above.

Swiss chard and aubergine lasagne

This is a very loose take on a lasagne that works well as an easy midweek dinner with friends. The tomato sauce can be made days ahead and kept in the fridge. In fact, I'll often double the sauce recipe and use it throughout the week for tomato pasta, spooned over meatballs (p123), or to top homemade pizzas. If you can't get Swiss chard, then substitute with spinach, cavolo nero, kale, mustard greens, spring greens… or whatever you fancy.

---

2 medium aubergines (eggplants), sliced into
    1cm/½ inch thick rounds

olive oil

2 shallots, peeled and sliced

200g/7 oz Swiss chard, cut into thick slices

175ml/6 fl oz/¾ cup white wine

100g/4 oz finely grated parmesan cheese
    or vegetarian alternative

2 balls mozzarella cheese, sliced

200g/7 oz fresh lasagne sheets

For the sauce

2 x 400g/14 oz tins chopped tomatoes

2 cloves garlic, peeled and crushed

2 tbsp olive oil

1 tsp balsamic vinegar

1 tsp caster (superfine) sugar

flaked sea salt and freshly ground
    black pepper

Time taken 1 hour / **Serves** 4

To make the sauce, put all of the ingredients in a saucepan, season with salt and pepper and bring to a simmer. Cook over a low heat for 20–30 minutes until the tomatoes have thickened (the time will depend on the brand of tomatoes as some are thicker than others to start with).

Heat your grill to high. Lightly brush the aubergine slices with olive oil and sit on a baking tray. Season with salt and pepper. Grill for 4–5 minutes each side until golden and soft.

Heat the oven to 200°C/400°F/gas 6.

Heat a good glug of olive oil in a frying pan and add the shallots. Sauté over a medium heat until lightly golden. Add the Swiss chard and fry until it is wilted. Pour in the white wine, then once it bubbles, season with salt and pepper and remove from the heat.

To layer up the lasagne, start with some tomato sauce in the bottom of an ovenproof dish. Then layer up in whatever order you like, until all of the ingredients are used up, making sure you finish with a layer of mozarella and parmesan on top of either the tomato sauce, aubergine slices or Swiss chard, rather than directly on the lasagne. Drizzle with olive oil, season with salt and pepper and sit on a baking tray.

Bake in the oven for about 20 minutes until the sauce is bubbling and the top is golden.

Flexible
You can make this in individual overproof dishes, so some can remain vegetarian. To others, you can add slices of sautéed or grilled chicken. Just layer the meat with the aubergine. Pre-cooked prawns or fried scallops would be equally tasty; simply layer in the same way.

Roast fennel and aubergine paella

I am a massive fan of Spanish food, and paella is my all-time favourite Spanish dish. I love the fact that there are so many regional variations, and like an Italian risotto, you can tweak it to suit your taste or mood. Make it vegetarian one day or add meat or seafood another time. For me, the best part is the layer of toasted rice at the bottom of the pan – it's called 'socarrat' in Spanish, and is considered a delicacy.

---

4 (approx. 200g/7 oz) baby fennel, quartered lengthways

6–8 (approx. 200g/7 oz) baby aubergines (eggplant), halved

1 red or yellow (bell) pepper, cut into 2–3cm wedges

1 medium courgette (zucchini), thickly sliced

olive oil

1 onion, finely chopped

300g/10 oz paella rice

1 tsp hot smoked paprika

decent-sized pinch saffron

200ml/7 fl oz/scant 1 cup white wine

800ml/1½ pints/3¼ cups hot vegetable stock

100g/3½ oz frozen peas, defrosted

1 lemon, cut into wedges

handful chopped parsley

flaked sea salt and freshly ground black pepper

Time taken 1 hour / **Serves** 4

Heat the oven to 220°C/425°F/gas 7.

Put the fennel, aubergine, pepper and courgette in a roasting tray. Add a glug of olive oil, season with salt and pepper and toss around to coat the veggies in the oil. Roast in the oven for 20 minutes, turning a couple of times until the veg are pretty much cooked through and turning golden.

Meanwhile, heat a paella pan or large frying pan over a low–medium heat and add a glug of olive oil. Sauté the onion for 8–10 minutes until softened. Increase the heat to medium and stir in the rice, paprika and saffron. Cook for around 1 minute to start toasting the rice, then add the white wine. Reduce by about half before stirring in two-thirds of the stock. Reduce to a simmer and cook for 10 minutes without a lid, stirring a couple of times.

Stir in the peas, add some seasoning, then gently mix in the roasted veg. Pour over the remaining stock, arrange the lemon wedges on top and cover with a lid or some aluminium foil. Cook for a further 10 minutes.

To ensure you get the classic layer of toasted rice at the bottom of the pan, increase the heat to high until you hear a slight crackle. Remove from the heat and sit for 5 minutes before sprinkling over the parsley and serving.

Flexible
Turn this into a seafood paella by omitting the roasted veg. When you add the peas, add around 350g / 12 oz mussels and / or clams, 150g / 5½ oz peeled raw prawns and some squid rings. Alternatively, for paella mixta, add a big handful of diced chorizo and 2–3 diced chicken thighs in with the onions.

Korean fried rice
with simple kimchi

Kimchi is a traditional fermented Korean dish that's eaten with almost every meal. It's usually prepared over a number of days, but I've done a simplified version that's quick to make, uses fewer ingredients and can even be used straight away. If you do have the time though, pack the kimchi into a large jar and leave overnight at room temperature, then store in the fridge and use within 2 weeks. Once the kimchi is made, the rest of the fried rice recipe is a breeze.

---

1 tbsp groundnut oil

3 tsp toasted sesame oil

100g/4 oz spring greens, savoy cabbage or kale, coarsely shredded

4 spring onions (scallions), finely sliced on an angle

2 cloves garlic, peeled and crushed

200g/7 oz cooked basmati rice

2 eggs

soy sauce, to season

1 tsp toasted sesame seeds

flaked sea salt and freshly ground black pepper

For the kimchi

1 Chinese cabbage, finely shredded

250g/9 oz daikon radish, peeled and grated

1 medium carrot, grated

2 tbsp flaked sea salt

3 cloves garlic, peeled and crushed

2½cm/1 inch piece ginger, peeled and grated

3 tbsp rice vinegar

2 tbsp sriracha chilli sauce

1 tbsp caster (superfine) sugar

Time taken 30 minutes + 1 hour salting and optional overnight fermenting / **Serves** 2

To make the kimchi, put the shredded cabbage, daikon and carrot into a bowl and toss with the salt. Leave for about 1 hour, giving the vegetables a little stir every now and then.

Meanwhile, mix together the garlic, ginger, vinegar, sriracha sauce and sugar.

Tip the salted vegetables into a colander and rinse under cold water. Drain well and shake dry in a clean tea towel. Transfer to a bowl and combine with the chilli sauce mix. You can either ferment overnight in a jar or use straight away.

To make the fried rice, heat the groundnut oil with 1 teaspoon of the sesame oil in a wok. Add the spring greens, spring onions and garlic. Stir fry for a minute or so until the greens are wilted. Add the rice and continue to stir fry until thoroughly heated through.

Meanwhile, heat a frying pan over a medium–high heat and add the remaining 2 teaspoons of sesame oil. Break in the eggs and fry until cooked to your liking. Season with a pinch of salt and freshly ground black pepper.

Add a couple of large spoonfuls of the kimchi to the rice, toss around in the pan and add soy sauce to taste.

Spoon onto two plates and top with a fried egg each. Scatter with the sesame seeds and serve with extra soy sauce.

Flexible
I really love the fried egg on top of this rice, and it's equally good topped with some crispy crumbed prawns. To make these, simply coat 250g/9 oz peeled raw tiger prawns in flour, then beaten egg, and then panko breadcrumbs. Shallow fry in sunflower oil until golden and serve piled on top of the rice.

Pasta ribbons
with sticky red wine figs, dolcelate and pecans

I'm a massive fan of pasta and could quite easily write a whole book on pasta recipes, but I've limited myself to just a few for this book, and this one was lucky enough to make the cut. I've taken one of my favourite ingredient combinations – figs, blue cheese and nuts – to create an utterly delectable dish.

---

8 ripe figs, quartered

125ml/4 fl oz/½ cup red wine

2 tsp red wine vinegar

1 tbsp runny honey

small handful fresh oregano leaves

100g/3½ oz pecan nuts

400g/14 oz fresh lasagne sheets

75g/2½ oz baby spinach leaves

2 tbsp extra virgin olive oil

150g/5½ oz Dolcelatte cheese

flaked sea salt and freshly ground
 black pepper

Time taken 30 minutes / **Serves** 4

Heat the oven to 220°C/425°F/gas 7.

Put the figs in a medium-sized roasting tray. Mix together the wine, vinegar and honey, and pour over the figs. Scatter over the oregano and season with salt and pepper. Bake in the oven for 20 minutes, turning and basting halfway through.

While the figs are roasting, put the pecan nuts on a baking tray and toast in the oven with the figs for 5 minutes.

Bring a large pan of salted water to the boil. Cut or tear the pasta sheets into approximately 2cm/¾ inch long strips/ribbons. Cook for about 5 minutes until al dente. Drain, immediately return to the pan and add the spinach and olive oil. Using a pair of tongs, turn the pasta to mix with the spinach as it wilts.

Break in small chunks of the Dolcelatte, add the toasted nuts, roasted figs and any roasting juices. Turn gently to mix and transfer to serving plates.

Flexible
Add some thinly sliced Parma ham or prosciutto to the baking tray with the pecan nuts, cook until crisp. Sit or lightly crumble on top of the pasta to serve.

Summary vegetable spelt risotto

The rich creamy texture of a classic risotto is one of my favourite comfort foods, particularly on a cold day. During the summer months, I like to swap the rice for pearled spelt and cook it with some fresh seasonal veg and herbs, which produces a lighter, more aromatic dish. Pearl barley also works, though it does take a bit longer to cook (about 35–40 minutes), so top up with more stock or water as required.

150g/5½ oz asparagus spears, cut into
   approx. 4cm/1½ inch pieces
150g/5½ oz shelled fresh or frozen broad
   beans, defrosted if frozen
150g/5½ oz fresh or frozen peas, defrosted
   if frozen
2 tbsp olive oil
40g/1½ oz butter
1 large or 2 small shallots, finely chopped
300g/10½ oz pearled spelt
150ml/5 fl oz/⅔ cup white wine
1 bunch spring onions (scallions), finely sliced
75g/3 oz finely grated parmesan cheese or
   vegetarian alternative, plus shavings
      to serve
1 tbsp each of chopped basil, chives and mint
finely grated zest of 1 lemon
flaked sea salt and freshly ground
   black pepper
extra virgin olive oil, to serve

Time taken 45 minutes / **Serves** 4

Bring 1 litre/1¾ pints/4 cups of water to the boil in a large saucepan, with a good pinch of salt. Add the asparagus and, if the beans and peas are fresh, add them here too. If you're using defrosted frozen ones keep to one side. Cook for 2 minutes. Refresh in iced water, reserving the cooking water. For a better flavour and colour to the finished dish, pop the broad beans out of their skins, revealing their vibrant green flesh.

Gently heat the olive oil and half of the butter in a large sauté pan or saucepan. When the butter is bubbling, add the shallot and gently cook until softened. Meanwhile, place the reserved cooking water over a medium heat and bring to a gentle simmer. This will be your risotto stock.

Add the spelt into the shallots and stir around for a minute or so. Pour in the wine and cook until it's been absorbed into the spelt.

Gradually add the hot stock, a ladle at a time, stirring almost continuously until the stock has been absorbed before adding another ladleful. After about 15 minutes, the stock should have been almost used up and the spelt tender.

Add the asparagus, cooked or defrosted broad beans, peas and spring onions and stir around until they are heated through, adding a little extra stock if the risotto seems too thick.

Mix in the grated parmesan, remaining butter, herbs and lemon zest. Season to taste. Cover with a lid and leave to sit for a couple of minutes before spooning onto plates or in bowls. Scatter with parmesan shavings, add a twist of black pepper and a drizzle of extra virgin olive oil.

Flexible
Shredded leftover roast chicken or shredded ham hock are both a great addition to this recipe. For a fishy twist, flaked smoked mackerel, smoked trout or hot smoked salmon also work well. Just stir the meat or fish through when you add the summer vegetables.

Turkish pide
with spinach and aubergine

*Pide (pronounced pee-day) is much
like a pizza, but has no tomato sauce
and a colourful, aromatic Turkish
flair. Traditionally, this boat-shaped
'pizza' is filled with vegetables, spices,
cheese and/or meat, most commonly
lamb. I've made this one into an
exceptionally tasty vegetarian version
using spinach, aubergine and feta, but
you can be as creative as you like by
using a selection of ingredients to top
the dough, as you would a pizza.*

7g/¼ oz sachet fast action dried yeast

1 tsp caster (superfine) sugar

300g/10½ oz strong white bread flour, plus
    extra for dusting

2 tsp salt

olive oil

2 medium aubergines, thinly sliced

1 red onion, thinly sliced

2 cloves garlic, peeled and chopped

1 tsp ground cumin

250g/9 oz baby spinach leaves

150g/5½ oz feta cheese, crumbled

1 tbsp sesame seeds

1 tbsp nigella seeds

flaked sea salt and freshly ground
    black pepper

small handful mint leaves

Time taken 1 hour + 30 minutes rising / **Serves** 4

Put the yeast and caster sugar in a small bowl with 2 tablespoons of
warm water. Mix and set aside for a few minutes until the mixture
starts to show some bubbles on the surface.

Put the flour, salt and 2 tablespoons of olive oil in a large bowl. Add
the bubbly yeast mixture and slowly add 170ml/5¾ fl oz/⅔ cup of
warm water while bringing everything together with your other
hand. If you feel it needs it, add extra water but take care not to
make the dough too wet. Once the dough starts to stick together, tip
onto a floured surface and knead for 6–7 minutes until you have a
smooth, stretchy dough. Transfer to a clean bowl, cover loosely with
cling film and leave to rise in a warm place for about 30 minutes.

Meanwhile, heat the grill to high. Brush the aubergine slices with
olive oil. Set on a baking sheet and grill for a few minutes each side
until golden. Remove from the oven and set aside.

Heat a glug of olive oil in a frying pan and sauté the onion for around
8 minutes until softened and golden. Add the garlic and cumin. Cook
for around 1 minute before stirring in the spinach allowing it to wilt.
Season with salt and pepper, remove from the heat.

Heat your oven to its highest setting. Divide the risen dough into four
pieces. Shape each piece into an oval, dust with flour and thinly roll
out. Transfer to a couple of baking sheets and prick the surface of the
dough several times with a fork.

Divide the spinach mixture and aubergines between the dough,
leaving a border around the edges. Pinch the ends of the dough and
roll the edges of the border over the filling, to form a boat shape.
Scatter with the feta cheese, sesame seeds and nigella seeds, drizzle
with olive oil and season. Put in the oven and cook for 10 minutes
until the dough is golden. Garnish with mint leaves to serve.

Flexible
*For a meaty twist on this recipe, omit the aubergine, and sauté around 200g/7 oz
minced lamb with the onion, continue to cook as above. Alternatively, to make this
into a seafood pide, omit the aubergine and mix 200g/7 oz cooked prawns into the
cooked onion and spinach before spooning onto the dough.*

Brussel, quinoa and sweet potato cakes

*These potato cakes are a modern take
on bubble 'n' squeak. They are super
quick to make if you have leftover
sweet potato mash or cooked quinoa
in the fridge. They're great served with
a simple chopped tomato and onion
salad, or some grilled tomato halves.
You could also pop a fried or poached
egg on top for added protein.*

200g/7 oz/1 cup quinoa (I like to use a
    mix of red and white)

500ml/17 fl oz/2 cups of water or
    vegetable stock

750g/1 lb 10 oz sweet potato, peeled and
    chopped into chunks

olive oil

1 large onion, finely sliced

250g/9 oz Brussel sprouts, finely sliced

2 cloves garlic, crushed

finely grated zest of 1 lemon

1 tbsp wholegrain mustard

1½ tbsp chia seeds

flaked sea salt and freshly ground
    black pepper

To serve

200g/7 oz Greek yoghurt

2 tbsp mayonnaise

finely grated zest of ½ lemon

handful basil, chopped

Time taken 1 hour / **Serves** 4

To cook the quinoa, heat a medium saucepan over a high heat. Add
the quinoa and toast in the pan for about 30 seconds. Shake the
pan to avoid it catching. Pour in the water or stock and allow to boil
for 1 minute. Reduce the heat to low. Cover with a lid and leave to
cook for 10 minutes. After this time, turn off the heat and leave for
5 minutes before taking off the lid and running a fork through the
quinoa to separate the grains.

While the quinoa is cooking, either steam or boil the sweet potatoes
until tender, before mashing and setting aside.

Heat 2 tablespoons of the olive oil in a frying pan and gently sauté
the onion for 5 minutes. Increase the heat, add the Brussels and
garlic and fry until the Brussels are tender, adding a splash of
water if they are starting to catch in the pan. Mix together with the
quinoa, mashed sweet potato, lemon zest, mustard and chia seeds,
and season with salt and freshly ground black pepper. Shape into
eight cakes and chill until needed or cook straight away.

Heat a glug of olive oil in a large frying pan over a low–medium
heat and fry the cakes for 2–3 minutes each side until golden. Mix
the Greek yoghurt with the mayonnaise, lemon zest, basil and some
salt and freshly ground black pepper. Serve a couple of cakes per
person with a dollop of the Greek yoghurt.

Flexible

*Serve these topped with some crunchy
grilled bacon or accompanied by sticky
roast sausages.*

Fennel, pumpkin and green olive tagine

A vegetable tagine is a great go-to dinner party dish as it can be prepared ahead of time then gently heated through when needed. This particular recipe is rammed full of spices and aromatic flavours, and I've also included some chickpeas to give it protein. It's pretty filling by itself, though you could serve it with some buttered couscous to soak up the juices.

1½ tsp cumin seeds

1½ tsp coriander (cilantro) seeds

2 tbsp olive oil

2 onions, chopped

3 garlic cloves, peeled and crushed

1 tbsp harissa

1½ tsp paprika

½ tsp turmeric

1 cinnamon stick

500g/1 lb 2 oz peeled pumpkin or squash, diced into 3cm/1¼ inch chunks

2 bulbs fennel, cut into thick slices, reserving leafy fronds if there are any

1 preserved lemon, finely chopped and seeds removed

600ml/21 fl oz/2½ cups vegetable stock

2 large ripe tomatoes, chopped

400g/14 oz tin chickpeas, drained

150g/5½ oz pitted large green olives

50g/1¾ oz dried dates, chopped in half

flaked sea salt and freshly ground black pepper

handful fresh coriander or parsley, roughly chopped, to serve

Time taken 1 hour / **Serves** 4

Heat a small dry frying pan over a medium–high heat. Add the cumin and coriander seeds and toss around until they start to release their aroma. Transfer to a pestle and mortar and coarsely crush.

Put a large casserole over a medium–high heat and add the olive oil. Stir in the onion and sauté for around 5 minutes until it's becoming softened.

Add the garlic, harissa, paprika, turmeric, cinnamon stick and crushed cumin and coriander seeds. Continue to fry for a minute or so. Stir in the pumpkin and fennel, until they are coated in the spiced onions, then add the preserved lemons and stock. Bring to a gentle simmer and cover with a lid. Cook for 15 minutes.

Add the tomatoes, chickpeas, olives and dates, and simmer with the lid off for about 10 minutes, until all of the vegetables are tender, and the sauce has thickened.

Remove the cinnamon stick and season with salt and freshly ground pepper. Garnish with fennel fronds/tops, if you have any and/or freshly chopped parsley or coriander.

Flexible

To make this into a chicken tagine, cut the quantity of fennel and pumpkin by half, then fry 6–8 halved chicken thighs when you add the garlic and spices. For a fish tagine, cut the fennel and pumpkin down by half, then add around 600g / 1 lb 5 oz diced firm white fish fillet (such as snapper or monkfish) to the tagine when adding the tomatoes.

Charred superfood salad
with grapefruit-spiked vinaigrette

Next time the sun is shining and you fire up the barbecue, give this recipe a go. All of the veggies can be cooked over the flames (or indoors on a griddle), served on a bed of quinoa and then given a massive lift with the grapefruit dressing. It's a perfect dish alone or to include as part of a feast when you next have a large summery gathering.

200g/7 oz quinoa

500ml/17 fl oz/2 cups of water or
  vegetable stock

1 butternut squash, peeled and cut
  into 1cm/½ inch thick slices

1 red onion, peeled and cut into wedges

200g/7 oz tenderstem broccoli

1 bunch asparagus, spears sliced in half
  lengthways if particularly thick

1 bunch spring onions (scallions), trimmed

1 large avocado, peeled, stoned and cut
  into thick slices

olive oil

2 tbsp pumpkin seeds

2 tbsp sunflower seeds

For the vinaigrette

grated zest and juice of ½ grapefruit

2 tsp honey

1 tsp wholegrain mustard

80ml/2½ fl oz/⅓ cup olive oil

flaked sea salt and freshly ground
  black pepper

Time taken 30 minutes / **Serves** 4

To cook the quinoa, heat a medium saucepan over a high heat. Add the quinoa and toast in the pan for about 30 seconds. Shake the pan to avoid it catching. Pour in the water or stock and allow to boil for 1 minute. Reduce the heat to low. Cover with a lid and leave to cook for 10 minutes. After this time, turn off the heat and leave for 5 minutes before taking off the lid and running a fork through the quinoa to separate the grains.

Heat a grill pan/griddle over a high heat. Coat all of the prepared vegetables in a little olive oil. Working in batches, cook the veg on the grill pan until they are showing deep golden char lines and are becoming tender. The times will vary on the veg, for example the butternut squash will take around 8 minutes and the spring onions around 2 minutes. If you feel they are getting too charred and not cooking, then transfer to a baking sheet and continue to cook in an oven set to 180°C/350°F/gas 4.

While the veg are cooking, heat a small frying pan over a medium heat and add the seeds. Toss around for a minute or so until they are golden and toasted.

To make the dressing, put all of the ingredients in a small clean jar, season with salt and pepper and shake well until combined.

When all of the vegetables are cooked, gently toss with the cooked quinoa and dressing. Scatter with the toasted seeds and serve warm or at room temperature.

Flexible
The options are endless for this recipe. You could incorporate some peeled raw prawns into the salad, cooking them with the vegetables on the griddle. Hot smoked salmon flaked into the salad is delicious. It also works well as an accompaniment to roast chicken (p173), slow roast lamb (p176) or duck.

dips
/bits

Labneh

Sometimes the simplest recipes can provide you with the most amazing result. What starts as humble yoghurt ends up as a luxurious Middle Eastern cheese that is wonderfully versatile.

This is a basic recipe that can be eaten with salads and flatbreads, drizzled with olive oil, spread on toast, used as a vegetable dip or crumbled over stews. It also makes a lovely breakfast or dessert served with honey and fruit.

To this basic recipe, you can also mix chopped herbs, garlic, citrus zests or spices into the yoghurt before straining. This creates some really interesting flavours. Have a play, and enjoy making your own creamy cheese.

500g/1 lb 2 oz Greek yoghurt or
 full-fat natural (plain) yoghurt
½ tsp salt

Time taken 5 minutes + 24–48 hours hanging / **Serves** 4–6

Mix together the yoghurt and salt.

Line a bowl with a piece of muslin or cheesecloth. Spoon the yoghurt into the cloth. Bring the sides together to form a tight bundle. Tie firmly with string, leaving a loop to hang.

Either thread a long wooden spoon handle or something similar through the loop and hang the bundle over a deep bowl or even over your sink. Or place in a sieve over a bowl. Leave the yoghurt to drain for 24–48 hours. The amount of liquid drained away will surprise you, and you'll end up with a thick and relatively dry labneh. Keep chilled for up to 1 week.

Tomato tofu sauce

This has become a firm favourite in my house, particularly with the kids. I started making it when I became fed up of them asking for (or demanding!) pasta with tomato sauce for dinner. As lovely as that may be, I became conscious that it wasn't really a balanced meal as it didn't contain any protein. So I came up with this recipe. They love it, and I love it because it can be frozen in measured portions making it a handy ready-meal. And as well as tossing it into cooked pasta, it can be used as you would any tomato sauce: spooned over baked potatoes, in a lasagne, as a pizza topper or even poured over nachos and grilled with cheese on top.

Time taken 30 minutes / **Serves** 4

Heat the oil in a saucepan and gently sauté the onion, celery and carrot for about 10 minutes until softened. Add the courgette, garlic and bay leaf. Increase the heat and continue to sauté for 3–4 minutes.

Stir in the tinned tomatoes, chilli flakes if using, balsamic, sugar, a good pinch of sea salt and black pepper. Bring to a simmer, cover loosely with a lid and cook over a low heat for 20–30 minutes until the sauce is rich and thick.

Transfer to a food processor, removing the bay leaf and add the tofu. Blend until you have a smooth creamy sauce.

Use straight away or store in the fridge for up to 5 days. Alternatively, you can divide the sauce into individual portions and freeze for up to 3 months.

2 tbsp olive oil

1 onion, finely chopped

1 stick celery, finely chopped

1 carrot, finely chopped

1 courgette (zucchini), finely chopped

2 cloves garlic, peeled and crushed

1 bay leaf

2 x 400g/14 oz tins chopped tomatoes

pinch dried chilli flakes (optional)

1 tsp balsamic vinegar

1 tsp caster (superfine) sugar

200g/7 oz silken tofu

flaked sea salt and freshly ground
    black pepper

The beauty of hummus is that you can add so many different flavours to the basic concept of blended chickpeas and tahini, whether it's using seasonal ingredients or favourite herbs and spices. Here are a couple of my favourite ones. Sweet Carrot and Harissa sticks with the traditional Middle Eastern theme, while Pea and Sorrel is wonderfully bright and fresh when lemony sorrel is in season. You could also try the same recipe with peppery rocket, watercress, basil or pea shoots. If these don't get you dipping your pitta, you'll find Roast Garlic and Lemon Hummus on p74.

Sweet carrot and harissa hummus

500g/1 lb 2 oz carrots

2 tbsp olive oil

½ tsp ground cumin

1 tbsp honey

400g/14 oz tin chickpeas, drained
    and reserving the liquid

4 tbsp tahini

1 clove garlic, peeled and crushed

1 tbsp harissa paste

squeeze of lemon juice

flaked sea salt and freshly ground
    black pepper

To serve

1 tsp harissa paste

extra virgin olive oil

sumac

small handful toasted pinenuts

Time taken 45 minutes / **Serves** 6–8

Peel the carrots and cut into thick batons. Place in a small roasting tray and toss with the olive oil and cumin, and season with salt and pepper. Roast in the oven for 20 minutes, turning a couple of times.

Drizzle the honey over the carrots and toss to coat. Return to the oven for a further 10 minutes until the carrots are tender and becoming golden. Remove and leave to cool to room temperature.

Tip the carrots into a food processor, along with the chickpeas, tahini, garlic, harissa and lemon, and season. Blend well until smooth. If the hummus seems a little thick, loosen with olive oil or a little liquid from the can of chickpeas. Taste for seasoning.

Spoon into a serving dish, swirl in the harissa, drizzle with some extra virgin olive oil, add a sprinkle of sumac and finally finish with a scattering of pinenuts. Serve straight away, or store in the fridge for up to 5 days.

Pea and sorrel hummus

400g/14 oz tin chickpeas, drained

200g/7 oz frozen peas, defrosted

1 clove garlic, peeled and crushed

15g/½ oz sorrel (when out of season try
    mint, basil, peppery rocket or watercress)

grated zest of ½ lemon

4 tbsp tahini

1 tsp agave or honey

2 tsp flaked sea salt

Time taken 10 minutes / **Serves** 6–8

This couldn't be simpler. All you need to do is put everything into a food processor and blitz until you have a thick paste. Taste for seasoning and serve straight away or keep chilled for up to 5 days.

Next time you have friends over for drinks or dinner, forget prising open a bag of shop-bought roasted nuts or crisps to serve with your G&T – have a go at making your own nibbles. These are both really easy and fun to prepare, plus they taste amazing.

Crunchy wasabi chickpeas

2 x 400g/14 oz tins chickpeas, drained

1 egg white

2½ tbsp wasabi powder

2 tsp cornflour

1 tsp salt

1 tsp caster (superfine) sugar

Time taken 1 hour / **Serves** 6–8

Heat the oven to 200ºC/400ºF/gas 6.

Pat the chickpeas dry with kitchen paper and scatter onto a baking tray. Put in the oven for 30 minutes, shaking the tray a couple of times throughout. Lightly whisk the egg white until frothy. Tip into the baked chickpeas and toss around to coat.

Mix together just 2 tablespoons of the wasabi, the cornflour, salt and sugar, and toss with the chickpeas. Transfer to the baking tray and return to the oven for 20–25 minutes, shaking occasionally until golden and crisp. Sprinkle with the remaining ½ tablespoon of wasabi for that extra fiery kick and leave to cool before serving.

Smoky maple spiced nuts

25g/1 oz butter

3 tbsp maple syrup

2 tsp flaked sea salt

1 tsp hot smoked paprika

400g/14 oz mixed nuts

Time taken 30 minutes / **Serves** 6–8

Heat the oven to 160ºC/315ºF/gas 3. Line a large baking sheet with baking parchment.

Put the butter, maple syrup, salt and paprika in a large frying pan. Heat together until the butter is melted and bubbling. Add the nuts and stir around in the pan to evenly coat in the sticky mixture.

Tip onto the baking tray and level out into a single layer using a wooden spoon.

Bake in the oven for 12 minutes, turning halfway through. Leave to cool completely before serving. As they cool they will become firm and crunchy.

Classic vinaigrette

A dressing can make or break a salad, and making your own from scratch needn't be difficult or time consuming.

100ml/3½ fl oz/scant ½ cup extra virgin
   olive oil
100ml/3½ fl oz/scant ½ cup groundnut oil
1 tbsp lemon juice
2 tbsp white wine vinegar
2 tsp runny honey
1 tsp Dijon mustard
1 small clove garlic, peeled and halved
sea salt and freshly ground black pepper

Place all of the ingredients in a screw-top jar and shake well. Season with salt and pepper. Taste and add any extra vinegar, honey or mustard if you think it's needed. The ingredients you use can vary hugely in their strength, so always taste as you go.

If you can, leave for at least 1 hour for the garlic flavour to infuse into the dressing. Store any remaining dressing in a cool place out of direct sunlight, but not in the fridge. Shake well before using. It will keep for weeks.

Tahini dressing

This is great with Middle Eastern-style salads – think couscous, aubergine, pomegranate, falafel, flatbreads, etc...

2 tbsp tahini
2 tbsp natural (plain) yoghurt
juice of ½ lemon
2 tbsp extra virgin olive oil
1 small clove garlic, peeled and crushed
6 tbsp water

Mix everything together. If the dressing is too thick, just loosen with an extra splash of water.

Keep chilled in the fridge. Use within 1 week.

Tofu, miso and ginger dressing

This Asian-inspired creamy dressing is lovely tossed into a noodle salad with raw veg. You can add it to an Asian coleslaw tossed with crushed peanuts, or simply drizzle over crunchy green salad leaves and crisp spring onion.

100g/3½ oz silken tofu
3 tbsp rice vinegar
3 tbsp white miso paste
60ml/2 fl oz/¼ cup water
2 tbsp pickled ginger, chopped
1 clove garlic, peeled and crushed
1 tbsp toasted sesame oil

Simply place everything in a small blender and blend until smooth, adding more water if needed.

Keep in the fridge and use within 3–4 days.

Roast tomato and basil pesto

In contrast to the two pestos on p165, this one takes a bit of planning as the tomatoes are slow-roasted in the oven to bring out their natural sweetness.

This pesto is a perfect partner for flatbread dippers, or as an alternative to tomato sauce on a pizza. You can also mix with breadcrumbs to top gratins or baked fish, knead into bread dough before baking, stir through couscous or top bruschetta and crostini.

---

8 ripe plum tomatoes

2 cloves garlic, finely sliced

2–3 small thyme sprigs

15g/½ oz basil leaves

50g/1¾ oz toasted pinenuts

50g/1¾ oz grated parmesan cheese or
   vegetarian equivalent

150ml/5 fl oz/⅔ cup olive oil, plus extra
   for drizzling

flaked sea salt and freshly ground
   black pepper

Time taken 1 hour 20 minutes / **Serves** 4

Heat oven to 120°C/240°F/gas ½.

Cut the tomatoes into quarters, remove the seeds and sit in a single layer on a baking sheet, cut-side up. Drizzle lightly with olive oil, sprinkle with the sliced garlic and scatter with the thyme. Season with salt and bake for about 1 hour until they are starting to wrinkle and looking dry but still a bit squishy.

Leave the tomatoes to cool, then put into a blender with the basil, pinenuts and parmesan. Pulse blend to roughly chop, then gradually add the olive oil until you have a chunky pesto consistency, but not a purée. Season to taste and serve.

Pistachio and kale pesto

The kale gives this pesto a slightly firm texture and healthy feel. Try it spooned over poached eggs on toast, tossed with cooked new potatoes, drizzled onto roasted vegetables or swirled into hummus.

100g/3½ oz prepared kale leaves
   (stripped from the stalks)
1 large clove garlic, peeled and
   roughly chopped
15g/½ oz basil leaves
50g/1¾ oz/⅔ cup grated parmesan cheese
   or vegetarian alternative
50g/1¾ oz shelled pistachio nuts
finely grated zest and juice of ½ lemon
125ml/4 fl oz/½ cup olive oil
flaked sea salt and freshly ground
   black pepper

Bring a large saucepan of water to the boil with a good pinch of salt. Fill a bowl with ice-cold water and set aside.

Put the kale into the boiling water and cook for just 1 minute. Remove with a slotted spoon and transfer to the iced water to instantly cool down.

Drain the kale and squeeze out the water. Put in a food processor along with the rest of the pesto ingredients. Blitz to a pesto consistency. Season to taste with salt and pepper.

Coriander, peanut and chilli pesto

This pesto is perfect for tossing into cooked noodles, spooning into Asian broths and spreading in sandwiches. You can also turn it into a salad dressing with more oil and some rice vinegar.

75g/2½ oz coriander (cilantro) (leaves and
   stalks)
50g/1¾ oz unsalted roasted peanuts
1 clove garlic, peeled and roughly chopped
1 long red chilli, deseeded and
   roughly chopped
finely grated zest and juice of ½ lime
100ml/3½ fl oz/scant ½ cup groundnut oil
flaked sea salt

Time taken 10 minutes / **Serves** 4

Put all of the ingredients, apart from the oil and salt, in a food processor and roughly chop together. With the motor running, add the oil to give a smooth pesto. Season to taste with salt.

Vegetable stock

You can buy some great ready-made vegetable stocks, but if you have some spare time then have a go making up a batch of homemade stock and freezing it in measured quantities.

Many vegetable stock recipes simply simmer veggies and herbs with water to make stock, but I like to sauté my veg before adding the water for an intensely flavoured end result.

_____

2 tbsp olive oil

2 onions, unpeeled and quartered

2 carrots, roughly chopped

2 leeks, roughly chopped

1 fennel bulb, roughly chopped

2 sticks celery, roughly chopped

4 cloves garlic, unpeeled

4 bay leaves

small bunch parsley

½ tsp black peppercorns

2 tsp flaked sea salt

Time taken 1 hour / **Makes** about 3½ litres/6 pints

Heat the oil in a very large saucepan over a medium heat.

Add the onions, carrots, leeks, fennel, celery and garlic. Sauté for around 5 minutes until lightly browned and starting to soften.

Add the bay leaves, parsley, peppercorns, salt and 4 litres/7 pints of cold water. Bring to the boil, then lower the heat, cover and simmer very gently for 45 minutes.

Have a taste and add more salt if required. Strain and leave the stock to cool before transferring it to containers to either chill in the fridge for up to 1 week or store in the freezer for 6 months.

Smoked red pepper, cannellini and walnut dip

This is a protein-packed snack, and also rather an impressive pre-dinner dip. To save time you can buy ready-roasted red peppers in jars. The flavour will be fine, but not nearly as sweet and intense as home-roasted peppers. (Picture on following page.)

---

3 red (bell) peppers

100g/3½ oz shelled walnuts

400g/14 oz tin cannellini beans, drained

1 clove garlic, peeled

4 tbsp extra virgin olive oil, plus extra to serve

1 tsp ground cumin

½ tsp sweet smoked paprika

1 tsp harissa paste, or more to taste

Time taken 30 minutes / **Serves** 6–8

Heat the grill to its highest setting.

Put the peppers under the grill allowing the skin to blister and char, turning a few times. Sit in a bowl and cover with cling film. Leave to cool for about 15 minutes before peeling away the skin and removing the core and seeds.

Heat the oven to 200°C/400°F/gas 6.

Scatter the walnuts onto a baking tray and roast for 8–10 minutes until becoming deep golden. Keep an eye on them so they don't burn. Remove and leave to cool.

Put the peppers into a food processor along with the roasted walnuts (reserving a few for garnish), cannellini beans, garlic, olive oil, cumin, paprika and harissa. Blend until you have a relatively smooth paste. Season with salt and pepper. Have a taste and add more harissa for a spicier flavour if preferred.

Roughly chop the reserved walnuts. Transfer the dip to a serving bowl and scatter the walnuts over the top. Add a drizzle of extra virgin olive oil and serve.

Beetroot and ricotta dip

You can make this using pre-cooked beetroot, but roasting your own makes this dip far better. Once the beetroot is roasted, making the rest of the dip is quick and easy. Serve with toasted pitta, breadsticks or crunchy veg. My favourite is leaves of chicory/endive as their bitterness works wonders with this slightly sweet creamy dip. (Picture on following page.)

250g/9 oz raw beetroot

olive oil

200g/7 oz ricotta cheese

finely grated zest of 1 lemon

½ bunch chives, roughly chopped, plus
    extra to serve

1 tbsp red wine vinegar

flaked sea salt and freshly ground
    black pepper

Time taken 1 hour / **Serves** 6–8

Heat the oven to 200°C/400°F/gas 6.

Scrub the beetroot and trim the tops and tails. Cut into quarters and sit in a baking tray. Drizzle with olive oil and season with salt and pepper. Cover with foil and roast in the oven for 45 minutes, or until completely cooked through, turning once or twice throughout.

Leave the beetroot to cool and then transfer to a food processor. Add the ricotta, lemon zest, chives and red wine vinegar, and season with salt and pepper. Blend until you have a thick dipping consistency. Have a taste and add more seasoning if needed.

Spoon into a serving dish and use straight away or keep chilled for up to 5 days.

Serve with extra chives and a twist of black pepper.

Perfectly cooked

/roast chicken

/steak

/pulled pork

/shoulder of lamb

/fillet of fish

Roast chicken

1.6–1.8kg/3½–4lb free-range or
   organic chicken
olive oil
55g/2 oz butter, at room temperature
flaked sea salt and freshly ground
   black pepper
300ml/10 fl oz/1¼ cups chicken stock
   (optional)

Flavours to add to the butter

- 3 cloves peeled and crushed garlic, 1 tbsp
  chopped fresh rosemary
- 1 tbsp paprika, finely grated zest of 1 lemon
- 1 tbsp garam masala, 1 tsp hot chilli powder
- 1 tsp ground cinnamon, 1 tsp ground cumin,
  1 tsp ground ginger and grated zest of
  ½ orange
- 2 tsp Chinese five spice, finely grated zest
  of 1 lime
- 2 cloves peeled and crushed garlic, finely
  grated zest of 1 lemon, 2 tsp dried oregano
  and 1 tsp hot paprika
- 1 tbsp ras-el-hanout (North African
  spice mix)

Chicken is an extremely versatile ingredient that can be cooked in almost any style and can take on pretty much any flavour thrown at it. Roasting a whole chicken is so simple to do: simply brush with butter and season well, follow the cooking method here, and the end result will be a succulent, juicy chicken that can be served hot or cold. You can also add all sorts of herbs, zests and spices to the butter giving you some amazing combinations to match dishes you might be making. The key is to buy the best-quality chicken and ingredients you can, for a superior flavour and end result.

Time taken 1½ hours / **Serves** 4

Remove the chicken from any wrapping, pat the skin dry with kitchen paper and leave out of the fridge for 30 minutes before cooking.

Heat the oven to 200°C/400°F/gas 6.

Add a trickle of olive oil in the bottom of a roasting tray, then sit the chicken on it. Brush, rub or spread the butter all over the chicken skin. Season with salt and pepper. Turn the chicken breast-side down, and roast in the oven for 40 minutes, basting with the butter every so often.

Turn the chicken over so it's breast-side up. Baste with the buttery juices and return to the oven for a further 20 minutes until golden. To check it is cooked, pierce between the thigh and breast with a skewer. The juices should run clear. If they are still pink, return to the oven for 10 minutes.

Transfer the roasted chicken to a plate, breast-side down, which will make sure the juices keep the breast meat really juicy. Leave to rest for 15 or so minutes. Turn the rested chicken breast side up to serve.

If you want to make the most of the flavour left in the pan, put over a high heat on the hob. Once it's sizzling, pour in the chicken stock, scraping the sticky juices in the base of the tray. Simmer for a couple of minutes, strain through a sieve and use to pour over the carved chicken.

Pan-fried steak

Indian

Seeds from 10 cardamom pods

1 tsp cumin seeds

1 tsp coriander (cilantro) seeds

½ tsp black peppercorns

1 tsp cayenne pepper

½ tsp ground turmeric

1 tsp flaked sea salt

Grind to a coarse powder

Cajun

1 tsp dried oregano

1 tsp dried thyme

1 tsp paprika

½ tsp cayenne pepper

1 tsp garlic salt

½ tsp ground black pepper

Simply mix everything together

Asian

2 star anise

1 tsp fennel seeds

1 tsp dried chilli flakes

6 cloves

½ tsp ground ginger

1 dried kaffir lime leaf or 1 tsp
    dried lemongrass

½ tsp black pepper

1 tsp flaked sea salt

Grind to a coarse powder

Moroccan

1 tsp coriander (cilantro) seeds

1 tsp cumin seeds

1 cinnamon stick

1 tsp paprika

1 tsp cayenne pepper

pinch saffron threads

½ tsp ground turmeric

1 tsp flaked sea salt

Grind to a coarse powder

There are so many different cuts of steak, each with a different taste and texture: rib-eye, sirloin, fillet, bavette, rump, onglet, flat iron… all are quick to prepare and cook. Keep it simple and flavour with salt and pepper or pick out one of the spice rubs below that is suited to your main recipe.

Spice rubs

All the recipes make enough to flavour up to four steaks (depending on size). Any leftover can be stored in an airtight container or jar. These rubs will all work well with lamb, chicken, pork and even meaty fillets of fish such as salmon, cod, haddock, tuna and swordfish.

To use, grind the ingredients in a spice grinder or use a pestle and mortar. Rub the steaks all over with some olive oil and then evenly rub in some of the spice mix. You can cook straight away or leave the spices to marinate the meat for at least 1 hour, intensifying the flavour.

How to cook steak

- Remove the steaks from the fridge about 30 minutes before you plan on cooking them so that they can come to room temperature.
- Heat a griddle or a non-stick frying pan over a high heat until it is very hot.
- Rub or brush the steaks with a drop of oil and season with salt and a little pepper. Quickly sear each side until deep golden.
- Continue to cook your steak by turning over every 30 seconds or so, until cooked to your liking.
- Based on a 2cm/¾ inch thick steak, a general guideline for total cooking time is as follows: rare, 4 minutes; medium, 7 minutes; well done, 10 minutes.
- If there is a piece of fat running along the edge of your steak, use some tongs to hold the steak vertically above the pan to brown the fat.
- Remove the steaks from the pan, place them on a warm plate and leave to rest for a good few minutes (this is essential) before serving.

Spiced maple mustard pulled pork

2kg/4 lb 8 oz piece boned pork shoulder,
    rind/skin removed
100g/3½ oz flaked sea salt
150g/5½ dark brown sugar
2 tbsp English mustard powder
1 tsp cayenne pepper
75g/2½ oz wholegrain mustard
75ml/2½ fl oz/⅓ cup maple syrup
150ml/5 fl oz/⅔ cup orange juice

For juicy, soft roast pork shoulder that effortlessly pulls apart, I like to roast it with the rind/skin removed. You can ask your butcher to do this, or do it yourself using a sharp knife, making sure you leave a layer of fat on the meat, and only cut away the rind in one piece. This can be rubbed in a little oil, scattered with sea salt and cooked rind-side up on a baking sheet for 40–50 minutes while the pork is cooking. You should end up with golden crunchy salty crackling.

Time taken 8 hours + overnight salting / **Serves** 6–8

The day before you cook the pork, put it in a dish or a large food bag. Mix together the sea salt and brown sugar and sprinkle all over the pork. Leave in the fridge overnight to draw out excess water, tenderise and evenly season the meat.

The following day, wipe all of the sugary salt off the pork and sit it in a roasting tray. Mix together the mustard powder and cayenne pepper, and rub all over the pork. Let the pork sit and come to room temperature for about 30 minutes.

In the meantime, heat the oven to 140°C/275°F/gas 1.

Mix together the wholegrain mustard and maple syrup, and pour over the pork making sure it covers the meat. Pour the orange into the bottom of the tin along with 125ml/4 fl oz/½ cup water, and put in the oven for 7 hours. If it starts to colour too much towards the end, cover loosely with foil. If the base of the pan starts to become dry, add a splash more water.

Remove from the oven and leave to rest for 20–30 minutes, loosely covered with foil.

Transfer the pork to a serving plate or board. Shred the meat into strips with two forks. Skim any fat off the juices in the pan and serve the juices to pour over the pork.

Slow-roast Middle Eastern lamb

1 shoulder of lamb, bone in, approx. 1.8–2kg
  (4–4½ lbs)
2 onions, peeled and roughly chopped
6 whole cloves garlic, peeled
juice of 1 lemon
4 tbsp pomegranate molasses
1 tsp ground cinnamon
1 tsp ground cumin
1 tsp ground coriander (cilantro)
1 tsp chilli powder
1 tbsp olive oil
flaked sea salt and freshly ground
  black pepper

To serve (optional)
handful pomegranate seeds
handful chopped fresh mint leaves
handful chopped pistachios or
  toasted flaked almonds

*There's nothing better than knowing you have a roast in the oven that's
doing all of the work itself – when it comes out, all you need to do is
present it at the table. The aromatic flavour of this lamb is just as
delicious when cold, so any leftovers can be enjoyed over a few days as
an accompaniment to many of the dishes in this book.*

Time taken 5 hours / **Serves** 6–8

Bring the lamb to room temperature by removing from the fridge
about 30 minutes before cooking.

Heat the oven to 160°C/315°F/gas 3.

Sit the lamb on a chopping board, skin-side up, and lightly score the
skin with a sharp knife. Scatter the onions and garlic in the base of
a large ovenproof dish or roasting tray and pour over 250ml/9 fl oz/
1 cup of water. Sit the lamb on top of the onions.

Mix together the lemon juice, pomegranate molasses, cinnamon,
cumin, coriander, chilli powder, olive oil, a good pinch of salt and
some black pepper. Slowly pour all over the top of the lamb.

Cover the dish or roasting tray with a lid or large piece of foil,
securing tightly. Roast in the oven for 3½ hours, then remove the lid
or foil. Continue to roast for a further 30 minutes for the top of the
lamb to colour, increasing the heat of the oven if you feel it could do
with more colour.

When the lamb has cooked, transfer to a large warm serving plate
and leave to rest for 20–30 minutes, loosely covered with foil.

Carefully pour any juices from the dish/tray into a bowl. Skim off
as much fat as you can, then pour the remaining juices back over
the lamb. Serve the meltingly tender lamb pulled apart into chunks,
allowing it to soak up the juices on the bottom of the plate. If you
are using them, scatter the lamb with pomegranate seeds, chopped
mint and pistachios or almonds.

Fillet of fish, various ways

Cooking fish is often much easier and faster than cooking meat. Use your local fishmonger, farmers' market or fish counter at your supermarket for the best advice on the type of fish in season and the best way to cook it. For no extra cost, they should also fillet a whole fish for you, and prepare it so it's ready to cook. They will also be able to advise on sustainable sources – sustainability is something you should be aware of as stocks of certain popular fish have been severely depleted by overfishing.

What to look for
Fish fillets should have clean, moist and firm flesh and shouldn't smell overly fishy. The fresher the fish, the better they look and smell. If you are unsure about the quality of fresh fish available, buy pre-frozen fish, which is usually frozen at its freshest. There are two main categories of fish: 'round' and 'flat'. Round fish sold as fillets include:

White Cod, haddock, hake, pollock, whiting, coley. Brilliant all-rounders; use any cooking method.
Pink Salmon, sea trout, trout, rainbow trout. Also perfect all-rounders; use any cooking method.
Oily Mackerel, sardines, herring.
When filleted, they are best griddled or pan-fried.
Warm water Bass, bream, mullet and snapper. Best pan-fried, baked or steamed.
Meaty Tuna, swordfish. Best griddled or pan-fried.

Flat fish include halibut, sole, plaice, dab, brill and turbot. They are often sold whole, but when filleted they are great baked, steamed or pan-fried.

Flavouring and portion size
When it comes to flavouring fish, it's best to keep it simple and let the subtle flavour of the fish shine through, particularly if you are serving it as an accompaniment to one of the dishes in this book, which will be packed with flavour. Season with salt and freshly ground pepper before cooking, then add a squeeze of lemon or lime juice once cooked.

As a general guide you'll need a fillet weighing 175–225g/6–8 oz per person for a main course.

Simple cooking methods
Overcooking your fish will make it dry and chewy. What you're aiming for is to heat the flesh all the way through and 'set' the flakes to keep in moisture. Look at the side of the fillet during its cooking time. If it's turning from translucent to opaque in the middle, feels firm but not yet flaky, it's time to stop cooking.

Pan fry Add a trickle of olive oil to a non-stick frying pan. Dust the seasoned fillet lightly in flour (for a light golden colour and to prevent sticking in the pan). Fry over a medium heat for 2–7 minutes, depending on thickness.

Griddle Pre-heat the griddle to very hot. Rub the fish with oil and season. Cook on a high heat for 2–6 minutes each side (depending on thickness), turning just the once. It should have deep golden grill lines on both sides.

Foil parcels Sit the fillet on a large sheet of foil, add a trickle of oil or butter, seasoning, herbs (dill, parsley, basil, coriander, tarragon or chives), and/or lemon slices. Wrap the foil around the fillet to create a loose fitting, tightly sealed parcel. Sit on a baking tray and bake in a oven set to 220°C/425°F/gas 7 for 10–15 minutes.

Bake/roast Ideal for thicker fillets such as salmon and cod that have the skin on. Rub with oil, season and sit skin-side down on a non-stick baking sheet. Bake for 10–15 minutes at 180°C/350°F/gas 4.

Steam Set a bamboo or metal steamer over simmering water. Sit the fish on buttered greaseproof paper, a bed of herbs or leaves (such as spinach, cabbage, banana leaf). Season and cover with a lid. Steam for 4–10 minutes (depending on thickness).

Index

creamy mushroom, leek and chestnut
      pie 102
   miso courgette noodle broth 55
   seeded wasabi tofu 90
   smoked tofu 99
   spiced tofu poke 105
   tofu, miso and ginger dressing 161
   tomato tofu sauce 154
tomatoes
   black bean chilli 107
   fattoush 78
   fried chickpeas, tomato and labneh
      flatbread 94
   paneer and turmeric corncakes 31
   radish and spring onion salsa 110
   roast tomato and basil pesto 162
   seasonal vegetable tarts 115
   shakshuka 37
   smashed bean, kale and tomato
      toast 72
   Swiss chard and aubergine lasagne 132
   tomato sauce 123
   tomato tofu sauce 154
   watermelon, tomato and hummus
      bowl 75
tortillas
   smoked bean mushroom quesadillas 28
   sweet potato and chipotle bean
      tacos 87
tray-baked summer vegetables 116
trout 177
truffle-popcorn croutons 53
tuna 177
   spiced tuna poke 105
   watermelon, tomato and hummus
      bowl 75
turbot 177
turkey
   creamy mushroom, leek and chestnut
      pie 102
Turkish pide 143
tzatziki 113

U

ultimate veggie burgers 119

V

vegan alternatives 15
vegetables *see also* peppers, tomatoes *etc*
   the green omelette 22
   smoky roots and brazil nut
      crumble 130
   spelt ribollita 59
   summer vegetable spelt risotto 140
   tray-baked summer vegetables 116
   vegetable stock 166
vinaigrette
   classic vinaigrette 161
   grapefruit-spiked vinaigrette 149

W

walnuts
   fig and goat's cheese salad 93
   smoked red pepper, cannellini and
      walnut dip 168
wasabi
   crunchy wasabi chickpeas 159
   seeded wasabi tofu 90
water chestnuts
   Chinese potstickers 67
watermelon, tomato and hummus
   bowl 75
whiting 177
wine
   pasta ribbons with sticky red wine
      figs 139
wonton wrappers
   Chinese potstickers 67

Y

yeast powder 15
yoghurt 15
   labneh 153
   tzatziki 113

Z

zucchini *see* courgette

Thank yous

I'd like to thank everyone involved who helped create this book, particularly my wonderful commissioning editor Zena Alkayat at Frances Lincoln, who got the wheels in motion in the first place. It has been an absolute pleasure working with you.

Massive thanks to Susan Bell for the stunning photography throughout the book. You have an amazing talent for making everything look effortless. Facundo Bustamante: not only are you a fantastic assistant to Susan, but such an enthusiastic foodie, which was a bonus!

Becci Woods – I can't thank you enough for assisting me on the shoot. You're such a great food stylist, hard worker and fun to cook with. Thanks also to Ella Hughes for the time you spent with us on the shoot. With an attitude to work like yours, you'll go a long way.

Thanks to Alex Breeze for the wonderful prop styling – you got it all just right. And to Canvas Home for the stunning crockery we used throughout the shoot.

At Frances Lincoln I'd like to thank Sarah Allberrey for design, Sarah Chatwin for proofreading, Hilary Bird for the index, Rachel Ng in production, and everyone in publicity, sales and marketing for getting the book out there for people to buy.

A huge thanks to my friends and family for being my chief tasters, and a special thank you to Phil, Olly and Rosa for putting up with the house being taken over during the shoot (and managing not to break any props… phew!).

Thank you to my super-agents Borra, Jan and Louise at DML – here's another cookbook to add to your shelves!

Last but by no means least, thank you to everyone who uses this book. I hope you enjoy cooking from it as much as I have enjoyed putting the recipes together.

Happy cooking everyone!